HOW TO
DOODLE

THE COMPLETE Guide

Kamo

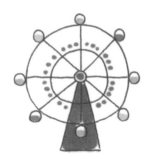

TUTTLE Publishing

Tokyo | Rutland, Vermont | Singapore

Contents

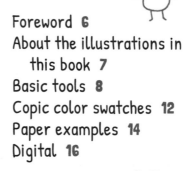

Animals and Living Things

People and Occupations

Food and Cuisine

Plants and Flowers

Special Dates and Events

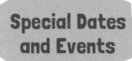

Houses and Interiors

Vehicles

Architecture

Weather, Seasons and Planets

Ruled Lines, Letters and Borders

Creating Characters

How to Doodle: The Complete Guide

Get ready for lots of cute illustrations!

Don't mistake this for a stuffy art tutorial! You can draw along with me or just enjoy looking at the illustrations in this how-to book. And don't worry about your drawing chops—this book is perfect for beginners.

Don't worry about realism or perspective; this way of drawing is about just finding one or two defining features to create caricature-style illustrations.

You can use ballpoint pens, markers or whatever drawing implements you happen to have on hand. They come in all different colors, thicknesses and drawing qualities, so see which ones you like best.

For those times when you want to try drawing; for those times when you're wondering how to draw something in particular; for those situations when you are required to draw something or for other random moments—I hope this will be the book you will turn to.

— Kamo, illustrator

About the illustrations in this book

Draw a basic line illustration.

Then, color in the illustration.

In other words, it's like a coloring book illustration!

Kamoko, your guide

Variations

Draw by mixing lines and color.

Or use only a marker to draw.

There are other methods too, so have fun drawing in your own way!

STEP UP!

In this book, Copic-brand permanent markers have been used. These allow for colors to be layered over each other, so give them a try when you want to take your work to the next level.

Second color applied after the first has dried

Gradation created by applying the second color before the first has dried

Basic tools

These are the basic items you'll need for drawing. I'm not particularly fussy about types of mechanical pencil leads, but I use different types for different tasks.

2B (Ain lead refills Stein 0.5 / Pentel)

This is my go-to lead. The drawing pressure required is just right and the paper doesn't get smudged with graphite.

4B (Neox Graphite 0.5 / PILOT)

Soft lead for when you want the pencil lines to show in the drawing. It has a good consistency.

HB (Uni Nano Dia 0.5 / Mitsubishi Pencils)

I use these harder leads when drawing a sketch that I plan to trace over with a pen.

Streeeeetch

As I don't like using plastic erasers, lately I've been using only kneaded rubber erasers. They don't leave crumbs, and they're handy to just fiddle with when you're thinking about something.

Kneaded Eraser (Holbein)

This excellent erasing tool can be kneaded into various shapes. There are many brands available.

Use half of the total amount.

Shape it into a cone for precise erasing.

Sometimes I form it into a cube or cylinder shape and just play with it.

Plastic Eraser (Tombow)

I don't often use plastic erasers, but when I want to completely erase something, I use this type. Mono is the brand I've been using ever since I was a student.

Personally, the item I get most nervous about when it starts running low is paper. Copy paper varies in color depending on the manufacturer, and the quality may also change when brands renew their stock, so it's a bit of a gamble. In this respect, Maruman Croquis books are consistent and reliable.

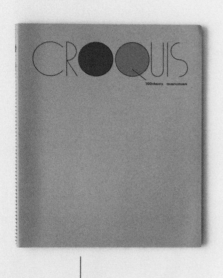

Croquis book (SQ size / Maruman)

I jot down everything in here, from rough sketches and ideas to journal entries and phone memos.

Copier paper

I use the lightweight type. It's a bit of a gamble buying paper, and I have tried plenty that didn't work out.

For drawing by hand, these types of pens are invaluable. The good thing about keeping these art materials handy is that no preparation is needed, so you can draw as soon as something comes to mind.

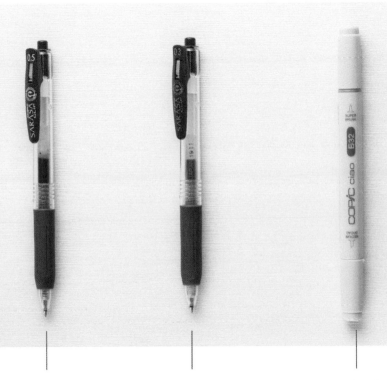

Zebra Sarasa Clip (0.5 / 0.3 mm)

This is a retractable pen, and I particularly like the range of available colors. For ballpoint pen illustrations, I use the 0.5-mm nib, and for drawing cartoons, I use the 0.3-mm nib.

Copic Ciao (2 nibs in one)

I use this Copic marker all the time. It's excellent for layering color. Copic's colors are identified by number.

Copic color swatches

The ink from permanent markers bleeds through the paper, so I recommend placing paper or something else underneath the page which won't matter if it gets marked.

These are Copic's 10 main colors, which the author has used in previously published books as well.

R46
(Strong Red)
I use this when
I want to make
a statement

RV42
(Salmon Pink)

YR15
(Pumpkin Yellow)
A shade like that
of a mandarin
orange

Y35
(Maize)
Soft yellow

G82
(Spring Dim
Green)
Light green
with a gray tinge

B93
(Light Crockery
Blue)
A stately blue

B97
(Night Blue)
A soft navy blue

V15
(Mallow)
Light purple

E31
(Brick Beige)
Light brown

W3
(Warm Gray)
Gray that tends
toward brown

Kamo's books published
by Tuttle

The 10 main colors that I use
all the time are the same as
those used in these books.

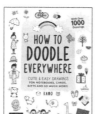

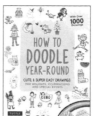

Here are 16 secondary colors. For the most part, these are intermediate shades of the main colors.

R05
(Salmon Red)
Close to vermilion

RV34
(Dark Pink)
Nearly-purple pink

V01
(Heath)
Pale purple

E04
(Lipstick Natural)
Red bean color

YG11
(Mignonette)
Pale yellow-green

YG23
(New Leaf)
Yellow-green

YG17
(Grass Green)

BG72
(Ice Ocean)
Green-tinged
blue

B32
(Pale Blue)

B24
(Sky Blue)

W1
(Warm Gray)
Light gray

W7
(Warm Gray)
Charcoal gray

Y21
(Buttercup Yellow)

YR20
(Yellowish Shade)
Cream

E11
(Barely Beige)
Reddish beige

E35
(Chamois)
Milk chocolate
brown

Paper examples

I keep a stock of blank notepaper and postcards. It's handy to have blank stationery because you can draw something different depending on the season, time, place or occasion. I choose types with simple ruled lines and that are a slightly higher quality of paper.

Things I've drawn

These are notes on which I've used a ballpoint gel pen or Copic Ciao markers to draw seasonally appropriate motifs.

▶ These are examples that I presented in how-to-draw videos in the Yahoo! Japan Creators Program.

Dear Mr. Minazuki,
I received some watermelon as a gift so am sharing some with you. Please enjoy it with your family!
From Hazuki

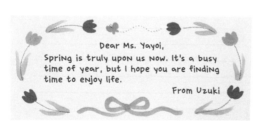

Dear Ms. Yayoi,
Spring is truly upon us now. It's a busy time of year, but I hope you are finding time to enjoy life.
From Uzuki

Dear Hazuki,
I hope the summer heat is not too exhausting. The osmanthus in the garden has a beautiful fragrance.
Please come to visit soon.
Nagatsuki

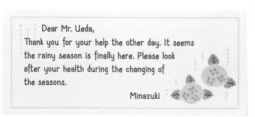

Dear Mr. Ueda,
Thank you for your help the other day. It seems the rainy season is finally here. Please look after your health during the changing of the seasons.
Minazuki

These are some of the notepapers and postcards that I keep on hand. There are various types, such as those made from Japanese paper, those where the lines are not printed but are raised or embossed into the surface, those that come with envelopes in a set and so on.

▶ Some are no longer available.

Digital

iPad

Some benefits of digital illustration
- You can easily duplicate your work
- You can share your work online
- It looks tidy and professional
- No drawing materials are needed

Drawing apps

Procreate

There are various apps available; I use the Procreate app a lot.

Benefits
- Can be opened quickly so you can start drawing right away
- Simple operation
- One-time purchase
- Has various brushes
- You can save your progress in stages

Drawback
- Only uses RGB colors

It's fun to be able to draw over photos!

It allows you to draw relatively detailed artwork.

Animals and Living Things

Popular zoo animals

Tigers

- Make the body larger than the head
- Fluffy neck
- Striped markings

Crocodiles

- Large mouth and protruding eyes
- Various triangles along the spine and body as well as inside the mouth

ENTRANCE

INTRODUCTION

Elephants

- Large ears and body
- Start with the ears to create a balanced look
- Make the baby elephant's body small

Bears

- The muzzle and large body are key points
- Bears look cuter without necks

Pigs

- Protruding snout
- Oval body
- Small, delicate legs

Pandas

Start by drawing a round face and ears.

Add thick forelegs.

Add the round belly.

Draw thick hind legs on each side. Add in the black fur.

Various poses

A caricature version is cuter than faithfully reproducing the real thing.

Eating

Walking

Playing

Lions

Make a guitar pick-shaped muzzle and add a nose and mouth; add eyes above it.

Make a V-shaped face and add two bumps for ears.

Add a full mane around the face.

Draw the forelegs.

The key points are the compact muzzle and large mane.

Draw a large body. Add the flared tip of the tail too.

Leave off the mane to make a lioness.

Giraffes

Taper the muzzle at the nose end. Add large ears.

Add the long neck.

Lower the rear end, creating a triangular silhouette.

Join the neck to the body
Lower the rear end to make a diagonal line

Long legs emerging from the body

The body markings are a key point

Chimpanzees

Use a horizontal oval and a heart shape to make the face.

The head is round. Use lines to indicate the fingers.

Draw large ears and a long arm.

The large ears protrude. The arms are lanky.

Add the long torso coming down from the raised arm. Draw one arm hanging to the side.

Make the legs short. Apart from the white areas, add brown fur.

Here is a chimp hanging from a branch by one arm.

Koalas

Draw a gum drop-shaped face. Add large fluffy ears.

Add the chubby limbs.

Give it a rounded back.

Koalas sleep a lot to devote energy to metabolizing the toxins in the eucalyptus leaves that they eat.

Here is the parent with a baby on its back.

In a tree

Koalas sleep for 18 to 20 hours a day!

Kangaroos

Draw large ears and the face.

Use relaxed curves for the back and belly.

Join the belly and back with the hind leg.

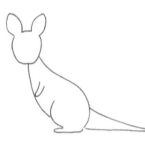

Add the foreleg and long tail. Show the tail resting on the ground.

Add the pouch and baby.

Use a different color for the baby to distinguish it from the parent.

Otters

Short limbs make for a cute look!

Draw a round face with small ears.

Add a long torso.

Draw the short legs.

Smiling face and long whiskers

Stoats

Summer coat

The color of the fur changes

Winter coat

Tail has a black tip

Draw a small face and small ears. Extend the long neck from the face.

Add a long neck and torso. Finish with short legs and a thick tail.

Capybaras

The positioning of the eye and nose is key.

The area below the nose is long. Add small ears.

Draw a rounded back.

Join the belly to the back.

Use a line for the narrow eyes. Draw in fur markings.

Animals that look slightly similar

Sheep

Start with a fleecy face.

Draw ears sticking out on either side.

Add the fleecy body.

Finish with hooved feet.

Lambs have only short wool, so use smaller curves for the fleece.

In the wild, sheep have long tails. Domesticated sheep have their tails docked for hygienic reasons.

Goats

Draw upright ears and a triangular face.

Add long, thin horns and a long beard.

Draw the angular body.

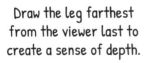

Draw the leg farthest from the viewer last to create a sense of depth.

Kids have drooping ears.

Newborn sheep and goats look very similar.

23

Popular pets  Cats

Strolling

Streeeetch

Various poses

Waiting for breakfast

Jump!

Lolling about

Different ways to draw cats' fur

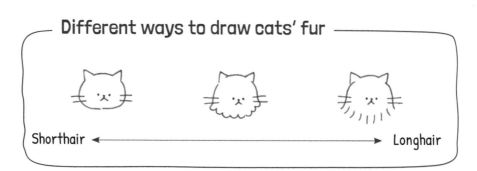

Shorthair ←————————————————→ Longhair

Various markings

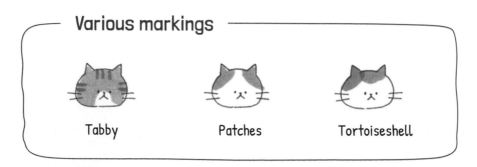

Tabby

Patches

Tortoiseshell

Munchkins

Its short legs make its
physique kitten-like
even when it is mature.

Tonkinese

This breed of cat has a
streamlined, slender outline
and build. Add dark color to
the muzzle, feet and so on.

Scottish folds

This breed is characterized
by ears that fold toward
the face.

Persian Longhairs

In this breed, the eyes and nose
are close together, making its
face look squashed.

Norwegian forest cats

This breed boasts a fluffy coat
and a thick tail.

Abyssinians

These cats are sleek
and wild.

Popular pets Dogs

Chihuahuas

This breed's ears stand out to the sides. Draw the lines representing the fur finely.

Pomeranians

It's fine to use a fluffy silhouette for the outline. Use about this degree of abstraction.

Miniature schnauzers

The mustache and eyebrows are charming features.

Dachshunds

These dogs have characteristically short legs and a long body.

A front-facing bull terrier

Various profiles

Large breeds with long muzzles

Small breeds

Long, slender-faced types, such as bull terriers

French bulldogs

Use a pear shape for the
drooping around the mouth,
and show large, upright ears.

Beagles

This breed sports a solid
torso, large ears and a tail
that arcs upward.

Toy poodles

Create an all-over
fleecy look.

Shibas

The outline of the
face is nearly diamond
shaped. The tail curls
back on itself.

Large breeds

Dalmatians

This breed has distinctive markings
and ears that hang down.

Dobermans

Note the triangular
body and pointy ears.

Popular pets (Small animals)

Draw simplified caricatures to create a chubby form with no tapering.

Hamsters

Make a tall, thin mounded shape. Create an arch for the feet.

Add small round ears.

Draw the small forelegs together in the very center. Add claws to the feet.

Add color and whiskers.

Rabbits

Start with a round face with long ears.

Create a rounded back extending from the face.

Draw a round tail.

Draw the hind legs to connect the tail to the belly.

Budgerigars

Draw an egg-shaped body beneath a peach-shaped head.

Add wings and a long tail.

Draw bumps for the beak. Make three lines for each foot.

Color in bright shades.

Turtles

This animal has a large shell. A large head looks cute.

| Make the end of the shell slightly pointy. | Add a rounded head. | Draw square legs. | Color in before adding cross-hatch markings. |

Telescope eye goldfish

Draw the body with curved shapes above and below.

Add a large eye.

Give the fins a dynamic look.

Add color. It's fine not to completely fill with color inside the lines.

Lionhead goldfish

Start with a large lump.

Keep the mouth in mind while joining the lines.

Add fins and a heart-shaped tail.

Color the head and tail.

29

Birds

Seagulls
- Round head and wings with rounded tips
- Gray and yellow are key colors

Parrots
- Prominent forehead
- Hook-shaped beak

Ducks
- Slightly large head
- Wide beak
- Plump body

Eagles/hawks
- Fringed wingtips
- Sharp beak and eyes
- Large, it's an eagle; small, it's a hawk

Swallows
The shape of the wings and tail are key.

Swallow chicks
- Only heads and bodies
- Make the beaks opened wide for a realistic look

Shoebill storks
- Massive beak
- Thin legs that look out of proportion to the rest of the body

Kingfishers
- Long, narrow beak
- Vibrant blue body

White swans
- Gently arched neck
- Base of beak is yellow, tip is black

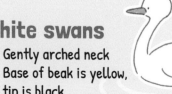

Flamingos
- Thick beak and long, gently arched neck
- Stands on one long leg

Insects

Spiderwebs

Ladybugs

- Round body
- Spots

Bagworm moths

Draw layers of frills with eyes on top.

Dragonflies

- Large eyes and thin body
- Bold wings

Cicadas

- Square head
- Brownish color

Praying mantises

- Large forelegs extending out to the sides
- Small triangular face
- Large whites of eyes with dots for pupils

Earthworms

One segment stands out.

Water bugs

- Forelegs for grasping prey
- Congregate in the water

Fireflies

Make the thorax red.

Water striders

- Entire body is long and narrow
- Lines for legs

Insects  Beetles

 Rhinoceros beetles

Beetles have a lozenge shape. Differentiate them by adding a horn or altering the shape of the horn.

Start with a semi-circular head.

Add a Y to a U-shaped abdomen.

Add six legs.

Alter the shape of the horn

 Make a small protrusion for a female rhinoceros beetle.

 Add a large horn for a male rhinoceros beetle.

 Extend the head to make a Hercules beetle.

Stag beetles

Draw the body in parts. Make the abdomen long.

Draw six legs coming from the thorax.

Add eyes on the sides of the head.

Change the shape of the mandibles

 Giant stag beetle

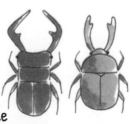

Sawtooth stag beetle

The colorful, glossy blue and purple types are particularly popular.

Papuakin Iron stag beetle

Butterflies

Cabbage white butterflies

Draw a rounded wing directed slightly upward.

Add the small lower lobe.

Draw the other side in mirror image.

Add circular markings to the wingtips and the middle of the wings.

Swallowtail butterflies

Make the markings distinctive.

Make the wing nearly triangular.

A section protrudes from the lower wing.

Draw the other side in mirror image.

Don't draw too many markings.

Morpho butterflies

Draw a line that extends from the body, and then returns.

The lower wing is slightly squared off.

Draw the other side in mirror image.

Color the wings blue.

Insects

Bees

| Draw a fleecy outline, and then add a circle. | Add a slightly larger egg shape. | Add bent antennae, and then add wings. | Add stripes and a stinger to the abdomen. |

Wasp

Large head

Danger

Nest

Paper wasp

Nest

Long legs

Grasshoppers

| Start with an angled head. | Add a squarish thorax. | Draw the thick back leg in the foreground. | Add the abdomen. |

Extend legs from the thorax. Add short, straight antennae.

Draw in a large eye.

Make the back legs large and thick, as they have the power to jump.

34

Sea creatures

Dolphins

Draw a long snout.

 Compare the dolphin to the killer whale to see the differences.

Draw the dorsal and pectoral fins facing in opposite directions.

Slightly slender form

Killer whales

Draw a short snout.

Draw small dorsal and pectoral fins.

Slightly thicker shape

Whales

Start with a bulging head.

Make the mouth large and open.

Add the spout and color the whale in.

Mammals move their tails up and down to swim, while fish move their tails from side to side.

Whales

Dolphins

People move up and down to swim too.

Fish

Sharks

Penguins

Start by drawing
a round head and
rounded wings.

Define the belly.

Add short legs.

The fledgling penguin's
body is roughly as tall
as its head.

The parent and
baby have different
markings.

Here's a chubby, cute
parent and child.

Polar bears

Draw a moderately
long nose.

Add a long body
and rounded rump.

Draw thick front forelegs.

Draw the nose larger than
the eyes. Add small ears.

A pose with the nose
protruding makes the polar
bear look more authentic.

Rounding the feet
creates the look of them
being covered by fur.

On the ice

Sharks

Hammerhead sharks
- T-shaped head
- Eyes at either end of the "hammer"

Whale sharks
- Wide head like a ladle
- Straight mouth and wide-set eyes
- Distinctive markings on back
- Longest fish body length in the world

Great white sharks
- Triangular form
- Two nostrils at the tip of the nose
- Back and belly are clearly delineated by color

Sawsharks
- Long snout like a saw
- Teeth along the length

Remoras
A small oval suction cup on the head adheres to a shark so the remora can tag along and share what the shark is eating.

Firmly adhered to the middle of a shark's belly

Sea creatures

The flute-like snout and tail curling to the front are key.

Seahorses

Draw the long snout and add the slope of the head.

Draw zigzag lines at the back of the head.

Draw a curled line coming from where the belly ends.

Add lines to the belly.

Cliones

Start by drawing a head like a cat.

Add triangular arms that extend as if cheering.

Finish with the body beneath the arms, tapering it like a depiction of a ghost.

The body is transparent, allowing one to observe the internal organs.

It's also known as a "sea angel"

Hermit crabs

Draw two large pincers.

Add long, narrow foreground legs. Don't draw them on the other side.

Draw a shell on the crab's back. Add eyes.

Color the shell any color you like.

Moon jellies

- Flower-like marking in the center of its bell
- Add lines from the frilled hem of the bell

Brown jellyfish

- Distinguished by its striped markings
- Many tentacles, some as long as 6 feet (2 meters)!

Spotted jellies

- Mushroom-shaped with polka dot markings
- Eight thick tentacles, like an octopus (only half are depicted)

Cassiopeias

- Shaped like a hand extending from a pond

Flower hat jellies

- Black markings on the bell
- Waving tentacles that glow green and purple at the ends

Spotted garden eels

Draw them all facing in the same direction for a realistic look

Sea squirts

- Semi-transparent

Creatures with the lower part of their long, slender bodies buried in the sand.

Deep sea creatures

Giant isopods

Start with a small
semi-circular mound.

Add a large mound that
flattens out at the base.

Continue to add mounds
of different heights next
to each other.

Add antennae
reaching upward.

Finish with
the legs.

Sadly, it can't
roll up like a
pill bug.

Footballfish

Start by drawing
a round body and
open mouth.

Use a rounded line
from the mouth to
complete the body and
add a rounded tail.

Draw a rounded body
with a protruding chin.

Add a
fan-shaped tail.

Add a fin on
the side too.

Add the "lantern"
and leave a spot for
the white of the eye.

Finish with zigzag teeth.
A subdued color works
well for this fish.

40

Coelacanths

Begin by drawing a wide open mouth.

Add a line for gills.

Join up the body, and then add the pectoral fin.

Draw a rounded tail fin.

Add multiple fins.

Add markings and leave a spot for the white of the eye.

Giant squid

Draw a partial triangle. Angle the bottom edges, but stop short of completing the shape.

Draw a long cone.

Add googly eyes.

Begin adding long tentacles extending from the body.

Add the two longer tentacles. There are 10 tentacles in total.

Add a person to indicate the scale!

Flapjack octopus ("adorabilis!")

Oh! I know that one!

Inspired by animation

Clownfish

Begin with a football-shaped body.

Add a small rounded tail.

Draw stripes.

Add largeish fins.

Finish by adding orange to the stripes.

Surgeon fish

- The tail and fins are yellow
- Slightly the distance eyes and mouth

Aquarium fish

Moorish idols

- Emphasize the long antenna-like fin and protruding mouth

Akashima white-whiskered shrimps

- Has a white line between red markings on the back
- Use lines to show the antennae and many legs

Porcupine fish

- Rounded body covered in spines
- Face looks cute from front on

People and Occupations

Family 1

Dad; mom; baby

The trick is to separate the thumb from the fingers.

Thicker neck than mom and baby

Round the shoulders and show the neckline for a feminine look.

Use a 1:1 ratio as a baseline for the chest and legs and alter to achieve the desired balance.

Make neck, wrists and ankles slender.

When wearing heels

Visualize the figure standing on tiptoes.

- Large head
- Short limbs

See also page 45 and pages 106-107.

Drawing the figure in profile makes it easier to depict a pregnant woman.

Babies

Wide forehead

Eyes appear half-way down the face.

Various expressions

zzz zzz

Women

The lower half of the face is bowl shaped.

Keep in mind the roundness of the head.

Various hairstyles

Men

Lengthen the face more than for a woman to create a distinction.

It's good to make the nose more prominent too.

Facial outline + nose + accessories

Family 2

Altering the head and body creates differences in adults and children.

Change the head and body to create various characters to match the feel of the illustration. For example:
- Figure two heads tall → cute character
- Figure six heads tall → mature character

For older people, raising the position of the shoulders makes the back look hunched.

Make the waist, wrists and ankles slightly plump.

Accessories are also key, such as a backpack for elementary school students and particular clothes for preschoolers.

For children from infancy to around third grade in elementary school, there is not much difference apparent between the genders when drawing them, so use clothing, hairstyles and so on to differentiate them.

Seniors

- Kind eyes
- Wrinkles around the mouth

- Make the hair gray, etc.

Various looks; accessories

Make use of hats, glasses and so on!

Toddlers

- Plump outline
- As for a baby, position the eyes about halfway down the face

Various looks; hairstyles

Try changing the shape of the mouth.

Elementary school students

- Face slightly narrower than an infant's
- For an immature appearance, position the eyes lower on the face

Various looks; hairstyles

Observe the children around you and refer to their appearances.

Family 3

Students in their teens

Middle school students

For traditional school uniforms and so on, rather than drawing them worn casually, make them look neat and proper to create the appearance of a student just starting at middle school.

Middle-school students' faces are not noticeably different from those of elementary school students, but they are taller.

Make heights and stances slightly different for girls and boys.

High school students

The body outline becomes slightly longer, with the physique similar to an adult's but slightly slimmer.

The casual way that clothes are worn (loose necktie, loose sleeves rolled up, etc.) differentiates the student from a businessman.

The relaxed way they wear their uniforms differentiates them from middle school students.

Faces turning in various directions

 Shift facial features to the top.

 Shift facial features to the right.

 Keep features in the very center.

 Shift facial features to the left.

Shift facial features down.

Leave the face facing forward and change the positions of the eyes, nose and mouth to direct the face in various directions.

Facing side-on

 Make the nose subtly protrude from a completely round face.

 Add hair, keeping the shape of the head in mind.

 Add one eye and the mouth.

Face slightly turned

 Make a slight indentation above the cheeks.

 The position of the ear is key!

 Add hair, keeping the shape of the head in mind.

 Place the eyes, nose and mouth on the side the face is turning toward.

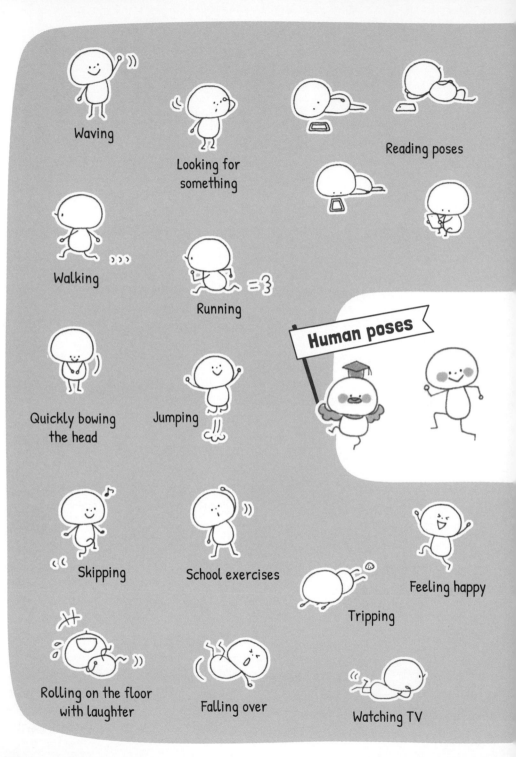

Waving

Looking for something

Reading poses

Walking

Running

Quickly bowing the head

Jumping

Human poses

Skipping

School exercises

Tripping

Feeling happy

Rolling on the floor with laughter

Falling over

Watching TV

Lifting something

Pointing in confirmation

Getting annoyed

Dragging something

Shivering

Use stick figures to check the poses! Then, add the appearance of flesh to complete the doodles.

The key to adding movement to a figure is to be conscious of the joints! Move around and observe yourself in a mirror to make it easier to understand.

Stretching legs out

Handing over documents

Checking out the situation

Feeling hopeless

Being tempted by favorite foods

How about an ice cream?

Feeling downhearted

Smiling nervously

Turning around

Sitting on the ground with knees drawn up

Carrying something home

Contentedness

Elementary school students' dream occupations

Popular with boys: Soccer players

Visualize a figure like this!

Make the arms reach out wide.

Draw the torso leaning forward.

Make the hips the center of gravity.

Draw the legs.

It's easy to make the pattern on the ball using a marker!

Popular with boys: Baseball players

Visualize a figure like this!

Cover the hand with a glove.

Bend the shoulder and elbow.

Make a deep bend at the knees.

Use the other leg to create balance.

Add your favorite colors to complete.

Popular with boys: Doctors

Visualize a figure like this!

Draw a white coat with a collar.

Draw one hand raised, holding a stethoscope.

Bend the hips to seat the figure in a chair.

Connect the legs and feet to the ground.

Extend the stethoscope tubing.

Occupations popular in recent years

Performers
Greeting the audience from behind a microphone stand

Hi there!

YouTubers
Bursting with energy

Popular with girls: Pastry chefs

Visualize a figure like this!

Start with a large puffy hat.

Draw the mixing arm bent at the elbow in the foreground.

Show the figure holding the bowl in the other hand.

Show the apron tied high on the waist for a more feminine look.

Add color at the neck and to implements such as the bowl for just the right amount of color.

Popular with girls: Nurses

Visualize a figure like this!

Draw a face with a cheerful smile and the beginning of a folder held at the side.

For a female nurse, taper at the waist.

Bend the elbow to raise one arm.

Show the figure standing with feet together.

Males do not have tapering at the waist.

Popular with girls: Nursery school teachers

Visualize a figure like this!

Start by drawing an enthusiastic smile. Add an apron.

Draw both arms outstretched.

This posture forms a welcoming pose.

Add the color or pattern of the apron and shirt.

Extras

Editors

← Cell phone

Illustrators

Occupation

tap tap tap tap

tap tap tap tap tap tap tap

Game creators

Line up several computers and use multiple "taps" to express busyness.

Popular uniforms

Butlers

- Air of politeness, necktie, vest and other neat clothing
- The eyes, nose and mouth appear low on the face to create the look of deference

Maids

- Apron with frill
- Frilled cap around the face
- Hands together in a deferential gesture

Pilots

- Double breasted suit
- Rounded cap with emblem

Police officers

- Trapezoidal cap
- Vest with multiple pockets

56

Shinto priests

- The tall hat and staff with paper streamers are key

Shrine maidens

- White kimono and red hakama pants

Flight attendants

- Scarf around the neck
- Neat, tidy appearance and compact carry bag

Geisha

- Long kimono
- Long belt
- Thick-soled sandals

Various expressions

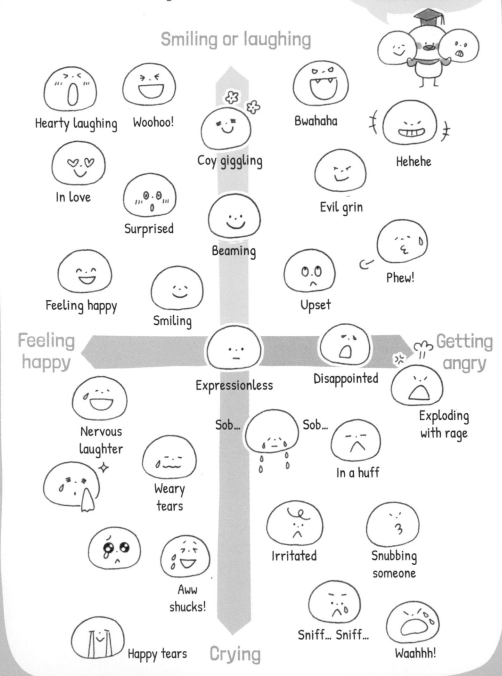

Pay attention not only to the shape and size, but also the positioning of the eyes, nose and mouth!

Smiling or laughing

Hearty laughing

Woohoo!

Coy giggling

Bwahaha

Hehehe

In love

Surprised

Beaming

Evil grin

Phew!

Feeling happy

Smiling

Upset

Feeling happy

Expressionless

Disappointed

Getting angry

Nervous Laughter

Sob...

Sob...

Exploding with rage

Weary tears

In a huff

Aww shucks!

Irritated

Snubbing someone

Happy tears

Sniff... Sniff...

Waahhh!

Crying

58

Food and Cuisine

Produce that everyone loves

Tomatoes

Differentiate between tomatoes and mini tomatoes by making the base pointed or rounded.

Start with a calyx with fine leaves.	Make the base of the fruit slightly pointed.	Leave a little white highlight when coloring to create a glossy look.

Pumpkins

Making the skin orange will create a Halloween pumpkin.

Begin with a horizontally elongated circle.	Add a thick stem.	Add lines and color green.

Sweet potatoes

< Split in half >

Make a marquise shape.	Fill with purple.	Add fine root hairs to finish.	Draw steam for a baked potato.

Produce that might not be so popular

Peppers

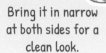

Bring it in narrow at both sides for a clean look.

Make bumpy lines for the top.

Draw both sides.

Make small bumps at the bottom.

Finish with a small stem and dimple lines.

Eggplants

The lines resemble the shape of a mustache.

Make a wavy line on both sides of the stem.

Make a zigzag line.

Make the eggplant plump.

Give it a glossy finish.

Leeks

Start with a long and thin stalk at the top.

Make two branches.

Use a rounded line to close off the base.

Add color only at the top ends.

Popular fruits

Bananas

Draw part of a
rectangle.

Make a shape like an
octopus leg for the fruit.

Draw about three
in a bunch.

Draw the creamy
interior of
the fruit.

Add the peeled-
back skin like
a collar.

Add color for the
unpeeled portion
of the banana.

One banana

Strawberries

Draw the stem.

Complete
the calyx.

Fill the fruit in
with color, and
then add seeds.

Cherries

Draw two
stems.

Add two similarly
sized circles, plus a
leaf.

One cherry

Popular mushrooms

King Oysters
Long, thin stem

Shiitakes
Chunky cap

Button mushrooms
Rounded cap; a cute, rounded form

Matsutakes
Rounded cap and a rough-textured stem

Straw mushrooms
Long, thin stem and small cap

Maitakes
Undulating cap shape that extends outward

Lion's mane mushrooms
Round and fluffy

Types of bread

Danish

Sweet bun

Chocolate coronet

Sweet bean roll

Sandwich bread

Dinner rolls

Baguette

JAM

HONEY

Rusks

Croissants

Place shapes like strawberries next to each other.

Start with a rounded triangle.

Add shapes on either side.

Add a little at a time.

Pretzels

Make an eyebrow shape with a thick end.

Draw a shape around it.

Draw the other end of the pretzel twist.

Leave the center open.

Sandwiches

Draw a triangle.

Use straight lines and wavy lines to indicate fillings.

Egg sandwich

Simply add filling to the right-hand edge of the sandwich.

Fruit sandwich

Cakes

Shortcakes

Draw a strawberry nestled on a mound of whipped cream.

Draw a triangle and rectangle underneath to form a wedge shape.

Add glimpses of strawberry slices in the cross section.

Apple pies

Draw the curve of the upper part of the crust.

Use lines to depict the thickness of the pie crust and add two apple chunks.

Draw a lattice pattern on top. Using brown is key to showing a realistic-looking baked crust.

Swiss rolls

Begin with a circle to show a cross section.

Indicate a generous swirl of creamy filling.

Add the side of the cake for three-dimensionality and draw a strawberry on top.

Baked goods

Biscottis

A traditional Italian sweet with almonds or berries baked in Add nuts to a long, narrow shape.

Stained-glass cookies

Use vibrant colors for the crushed candies that are added before baking.

Cookies

Use various shapes such as squares and circles.

Digestive biscuits

Use bumpy lines for the outline and add dots to the center.

Bonbons/chocolates

Chocolate shells with fillings. Draw the cross section for a realistic look.

Muffins

Draw the top so that it is nearly spilling over the cup.

Crêpes

Draw folded triangles to form the traditional look.

67

Japanese sweets

Dorayaki

Start by drawing the seams at the sides.

Join the seams with a rounded top.

Make a shallow bottom section and add a line to define the center.

Indicate filling in the cross section.

O-dango rice dumplings

Draw three circles.

Add a line for a skewer, as if it is passing through them.

Three-colored *dango*.

Dango with a sweet soy glaze.

Ichigo daifuku

Bean jam around the strawberry

Draw a plump circle shape.

Add a rounded triangle shape for a strawberry slice.

Depicted here are bean *daifuku* and mugwort *daifuku* distinguished by color and addition of beans.

68

Japanese cuisine

Oden stew

Fish paste

Kombu

Flour paste cake

Tofu and vegetables

Egg

Daikon

Konjac

Pounded fish cake

Frankfurter Sausage

Octopus

Beef

Fried tofu

Rice

Miso soup

Pickles

World cuisine

Steak

Begin by
drawing a long
oval shape.

Indicate
thickness.

Add
accompaniments
and grill marks.

Steak plate

Cabbage rolls

Begin with a
packet shape.

Draw a string wrapped
around the packet.

Add
accompaniments
and leaf details.

Add color for soup.

Knife   Fork   Spoon

Chinese cuisine

Ramen

Draw an oval and add the side of the bowl and its base.

Add fish paste and an egg (cut in half).

Use curved lines for the noodles.

Add soup and steam. Add color, and don't forget to include the soup spoon.

Gyoza

Draw a crescent moon shape.

Add another line to indicate thickness.

Line the dumplings up on a plate.

Shumai

Wonton

Xiao long bao

Steamed meat bun

Food to go

Hot dogs

Draw a
sausage.

Show it nestled
in a roll.

Add ketchup.

Hamburgers

Begin with a dome-
shaped bun top.

Add the patty
and fixings.

Draw a horizontal
rectangle for the
bottom bun.

Side menu

Beverages

Soft-serve ice cream

Biscuits

Fries

Chicken nuggets

Onion rings

Old-school café menu

Spaghetti Napolitana
Depict orange-colored spaghetti with chopped vegetables throughout.

Curries
Use curved lines for the outline of the sauce, and bumpy lines for the rice.

Omelettes
Draw an almond shape for the egg portion and indicate plenty of sauce. Add parsley if you wish.

Pizza toasts
Draw a slice of Texas toast with red, yellow and green toppings.

Hotcakes
Make a stack of two hotcakes and show a pat of butter on top.

Parfaits
Draw it from the side so the layers are clearly visible.

Soft drinks

Bubble teas

Start by drawing
the edge of the lid
like a railway track.

Add a
trapezoid below.

Draw a thick straw.

Finish by
indicating large
tapioca balls.

Coffees & lattes

Begin by drawing
an oval shape.

Make the side rounded.
Add a handle.

Show the cup only
half full of coffee.

For a latte, make the
cup nearly full and
add a swirl motif.

Cream sodas

Taper the mouth
of the glass.

Add a round scoop
of ice cream.

Add a cherry
on top.

Leave areas white
when adding color
to indicate ice.

Alcoholic beverages

Beer

In a beer mug

Rather than coloring in the entire mug edge to edge, leave a gap around the outside to create the look of thick glass.

In a can

Add foam to make it clear that it's beer.

Beer

Add lettering if you like.

Common alcoholic drinks

Cocktails & Wine

Glasses with long, fine stems

Whiskey

Draw a large block of ice for whiskey on the rocks.

Saké

Bottle and cup set

Labels with English lettering

Substantial bottle

A vertical label makes for an authentic look.

Making vegetables look stylish

Peppers

Use only color (no lines) for these stylish vegetables to give them an elegant, simple look.

Color a long narrow oval in the center.

Add another long narrow oval on the left.

Add another long narrow oval on the right.

Avocados

Color in an oval.

Add skin surrounding the shape and the large round seed.

Cilantro

Add the stem for an authentic look.

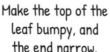
Make the top of the leaf bumpy, and the end narrow.

Draw the same basic shape again underneath.

Draw a third shape to create one cluster of leaves.

Plants and Flowers

Birth month flowers

Stack the flowers to form a stem.

Boat orchids (Cymbidium)

Make a puffy popcorn shape that is slightly pointed at the base.

Add a petal at the top.

Add petals on either side and two larger petals beneath those.

The long, narrow leaves are straight and extend upward.

[February] **Freesias**

Draw three rounded points for petals.

Add rounded points between the first petals.

Add flowers horizontally along the branch.

Extend a branch horizontally, and add buds of different sizes coming off the top.

Add a long stem.

Finish with long, narrow leaves.

Valentine's Day flowers; flowers that symbolize love

Anemones

Draw lines extending from a circle.

Add puffy petals.

Draw a long stem.

Draw leaves with wavy edges directly below the flower.

Leave white around the center of the flower.

Sweet pea flowers

Draw a small triangle at the end of a curved stem.

Add a flower shaped like a heart on its side.

Add flowers along the stem.

Color pale pink, purple, etc.

It's easiest to draw these as if viewing the flowers from the side.

[March] Tulips

Make it simple with a plump flower and large, broad leaves.

Begin by drawing a teardrop-shaped petal.

Make the blossom plump at the sides by adding more petals.

Draw a long stem.

Draw a large, broad leaf at the base.

Add another leaf.

Make it even simpler by only using one line to draw the entire blossom.

[April] Cherry blossoms (sakura)

Start by drawing a petal that's left open at the base.

Complete 5 petals for the standard flower.

Add the center to complete one blossom.

Many sakura flowers clustered on the one branch

Scattered petals

[Flower arranging]

Nosegays

- Bundle together flowers with long stems
- Widen the wrapping paper section
- Make the flowers and stalks protrude from the top for a gorgeous effect

Bouquets

- Has an overall rounded look
- Make the flowers large and place them densely together for an attractive presentation

The trick to a good result is making the flowers large!

Floral arrangements

Place flowers and leaves in a basket or planter.

Herbariums

Meaning "botanical specimen," this refers to flowers in bottles of oil. Use your imagination to create a transparent bottle with flowers and leaves Add a tag or ribbon for a cute touch!

[May] Lilies of the valley

Draw a large leaf.

Add a curved stem.

Add a rounded flower.

Add a few flower
stalks (peduncles).

Add the rest of the flowers.
Color only the leaves and
the tips of the petals.

[June] Roses

Begin with a rounded
diamond shape.

Join the centers
of two sides.

Repeat at
the top.

Continue until you
reach the center.

Complete.
Add four triangular
petals around the edge.

Finish with a long
stem and thorns.

It's easier to make divisions
within a shape than to draw each
individual petal.

82

[Mother's Day · Father's Day]

Mother's Day: carnations

Make the top of the center petal jagged.

Add petals to the sides.

Add two large petals on top.

Create a domed shape.

Add a rounded calyx and the stem.

Finish with narrow leaves.

How to make a simple card

▶ Yellow roses are a traditional choice for Father's Day.

1. Leave a white border around the illustration and cut it out.
2. Write a message on the back.
3. Draw a ribbon tied onto the stem to complete the card.

Draw a curved cone.   Add flanking curved cones.   Make a total of 6.

Add a long triangle.

This blossom consists of a long trumpet shape with curled petals.

Finish with a long stem and leaves.

[August] **Sunflowers**

Draw a large circle.   Add long narrow petals around the edge.

Add a long stem with large leaf.   Add color.   Fill in seed detail to complete.

[Plants that flower around the mid-summer Bon festival]

Chinese lantern plants

Draw a leaf with
a pointed tip.

Extend the stem
past the second leaf.

Add a pod with
a narrowed tip.

Repeat.

Add color.

Gentians

Begin with a
star shape.

Add an inverted
triangle.

Add a second blossom
and a closed bud.

Extend a
long stem.

Finish with
leaves, and
then add
color.

Draw a shape with small bumps.

Add a bumpy shape around it.

Add another bumpy shape around that to complete the petals.

The bumpy outline of the petals is key!

Extend a long stem.

Add leaves and then color.

[October] **Gerberas**

Start by drawing a bumpy shape.

Draw a circle in the center.

Add long, narrow petals all around.

When changing the angle...

Make the center an oval.

Make the petals at the back short.

Make the petals at the front long.

86

[Bonsai]

Coniferous trees

Make a bent trunk and add green glove-shaped tufts.

Pine and oak trees are popular bonsai choices.

Foliage trees

Draw red and yellow leaves. Use the curved branches and mounded soil to create a classic bonsai look. Use all light green leaves create a summer version.

Flowering trees

Draw flowers in a cluster. Scattering a few petals is key.

Fruiting trees

Feature a thick, straight trunk with small fruits.

Twisting the branches makes for a realistic bonsai look!

Kokedama (moss balls)

Cover a ball of soil with moss and add leaves sprouting from the top.

[November] **Cyclamens**

Draw a short
straight line.

Add three large
petals above it.

Add a supple stem.

Draw heart-shaped
leaves.

Color the leaves,
leaving white sections
to form the patterns.

The turned-back
petals characterize
a cyclamen.

[December] **Poinsettias**

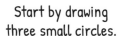

Start by drawing
three small circles.

Add leaf-like shapes.

Add three more
leaves between
those from the
previous step.

Add circles in between
the other circles.

Color, and then
add leaf vein lines.

[Mushrooms]

Amanita muscaria

- Typical toxic red toadstools like the ones in fairytales
- Leave white spots when coloring

Death caps

A poisonous mushroom characterized by a yellow color like that of an egg yolk.

Amanita virgineoides

- Cap like a rounded mountain
- Pointy white protrusions
- Stem is large around the base

Mycena pura

- A purple poisonous mushroom
- Deepen color at the top
- Make the stem long and thin

Omphalotus japonicus

- Similar to shiitakes in shape
- Because it glows in the, dark, it's fine to just use one color

Stages of mushroom growth

Depict the cap gradually opening out as the fungus matures. (There are some exceptions to the rule.)

Plants that you want to touch

Mimosas

When touched, the stem lowers as if the plant is bowing.

Start by drawing a large oval.

Add slightly smaller ovals.

Draw a pink circle.

Add detail lines to the flower and leaves.

Crape myrtles

Begin by drawing small circles for the center.

Join a petal to each circle.

Here, the pointed seed pod has been added. When handled, the seed inside pops out.

Draw three heart-shaped leaves, and then add color.

Carnivorous plants

Venus flytraps

Start by drawing a bean-like shape.

Indicate the superimposed half.

Add leaves.

Add multiple lines for the bristles.

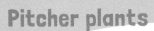

Color the interior purple.

Pitcher plants

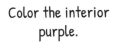

Begin by drawing a teardrop shape.

Make the base taper and curve.

Add a curling vine.

Complete the drawing with a lid.

Use reddish and greenish tones for contrast.

Plants grown at school

Use lines and color separately for a professional-looking effect.

Morning Glories

Fill a large circle with five areas of color.

Add a triangle to make a trumpet shape.

Add the distinctive leaf.

Draw the curly vine and color in the leaf.

Hyacinths

Use a marker to draw a little six-petal flower (this illustration doesn't feature pen outlines).

Visualize the overall shape as an elongated oval.

Use the marker to draw a cluster of flowers.

Finish with long, slender leaves emerging from the base.

Special Dates
and Events

January

For this talisman, draw the left eye to make a wish and fill in the right eye when it comes true.

Daruma

Draw as if making a circle, with the base tapered.

Leave white for the face.

New-Year's rice cakes

Stack mounded rice cakes and join diamond shapes for the paper decorations.

New-Year's pine decorations

Indicate the nodes in the bamboo stalks.

Beckoning cats (maneki neko)

Make the ears slightly broad and round off the paw.

Round off the hind legs as well for a cute look.

If the right paw of this talisman is raised, it is to attract money, while if the left paw is raised, it is to attract companions.

February

Sushi

Draw a slightly flattened oval.

Extend it out to the side to make it three-dimensional.

Use color to indicate the fillings.

Evil spirits

Begin by drawing curly hair, like a cloud, and a bowl-shaped face.

Add small horns and facial features.

Draw one arm extended.

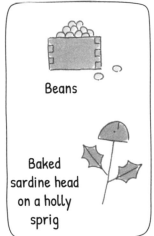

Beans

Add a loincloth with a jagged hem and set the legs wide to indicate an imposing stance.

Finish by adding a metal club.

These are items to ward off evil spirits.

Baked sardine head on a holly sprig

March

Doll festival Make round faces for the dolls for a kind, adorable look.

Emperor   Empress

Three court attendants

Kuwae no Choshi   Sanpo   Nagae no Choshi

Five court musicians

Hand drum   Large drum   Small drum   Flute   Noh chanting

The farther to the left the musician appears, the louder their instrument is.

▶ The positioning of the dolls varies by region in Japan.

April

Cherry blossoms

Draw a large
fluffy cloud.

Add a trunk with
horizontal markings.

Draw outsized
cherry blossoms.

Paper lanterns

Start by drawing a
rectangle at the top.

Add the sides.

Add a rectangle at
the bottom.

Indicate the
distinctive stripes.

Easter Bunnies

Begin by drawing
the outline of the
head at the sides.

Draw three flowers
on top of the head.

Add long ears.

Place the bunny in
a colorful egg for a
festive motif.

May

Carp banners

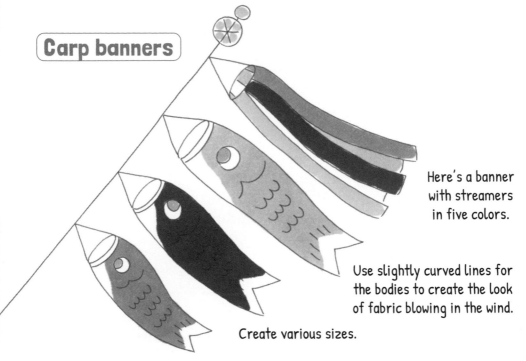

Here's a banner with streamers in five colors.

Use slightly curved lines for the bodies to create the look of fabric blowing in the wind.

Create various sizes.

Samurai helmets

Make the part of the interior that's visible by drawing a long leaf shape.

Make large horns; these can be various shapes.

Make the mounded crown section.

Add rectangles on the sides.

Add the tied chin strap.

Add the color scheme.

98

June

Hydrangeas

Begin by drawing a large circle.

Add small flowers with four petals.

Add large leaves.

If the soil is acidic, the flowers will be blue.

If the soil is neutral to alkaline, the flowers are pink.

Frogs

Make a circle with a flattened base.

Add two large eyes.

Add an egg-shaped body.

Define the legs.

Indicate the toes and add a big mouth and nostrils.

July

Long narrow leaves

Show hanging strips of wishing paper, etc., suspended by string.

It is said that it is better to wish for a specific thing to improve, not for an item you desire.

Branches emerging from nodes on the trunk

Cowherds & Weaver girls

Draw a single bun atop a rounded, squareish face with ears.

Have the kimono sides overlap in a Y shape.

Finish by using two ovals to indicate crossed legs.

Make a heart shape with two openings atop the head.

Add facial features and the belt tied in front.

Make the hem of the kimono look organic.

100

August

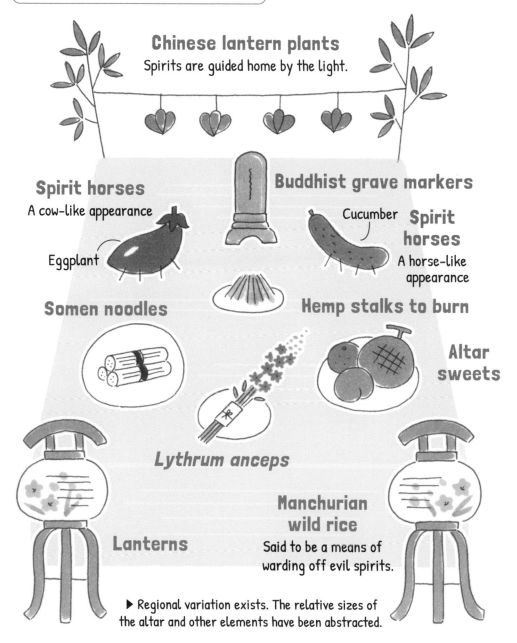

Chinese lantern plants
Spirits are guided home by the light.

Spirit horses
A cow-like appearance

Eggplant

Buddhist grave markers

Cucumber **Spirit horses**
A horse-like appearance

Somen noodles

Hemp stalks to burn

Altar sweets

Lythrum anceps

Lanterns

Manchurian wild rice
Said to be a means of warding off evil spirits.

▶ Regional variation exists. The relative sizes of the altar and other elements have been abstracted.

101

September

Moon-viewing decorations

Miscanthus sinensis
- One of the seven herbs of fall, said to ward off evil
- Make the ends fluffy

Moon

In Japan, it's said if you look at the moon, you can see the figure of a rabbit pounding rice.

Moon viewing dumplings
- Symbolize the full moon
- Stack them in three layers

Grapes
Vines are auspicious as they connect people with the moon.

Saké
Draw the bottle and cup together as a set for a realistic look.

Taro
A traditional choice to celebrate the potato harvest.

October (Halloween)

Jack-o'-lanterns
- Wide open eyes and mouth
- Draw the vine of the pumpkin too if you like

Skulls
Draw this spooky motif so it has a bulbous cranium and large eye sockets.

Vampires
Give him fangs and a long coat.

Candies

Ghosts
Taper the base to a point.

Bats

Draw pointy triangular ears.

Make peaks in the top of the wings.

Use wavy lines for the bottom of the wings.

Witches

November (Shichi-Go-San festival)

Three-year-olds

Start by drawing the large hair decoration. Add ornaments to the vest.

Continue drawing the outfit. Extend both arms in a natural pose.

Show a little of the kimono peeking out from underneath and add color.

Five-year-olds

Traditional *chitose-ame* candy

Make the *haori* jacket long.

Use a trapezoid for the hakama pants.

Place the legs apart for a wide stance.

Seven-year-olds

Draw the head, upper body, and trailing hair ornaments.

Complete the kimono as rectangle.

Show the *obi* belt tied behind. Add gorgeous color.

December

Christmas

Reindeer
- Long antlers, solid body
- Fluffy around the neck

Christmas trees
- Stack triangles to make the silhouette
- Decorate as you like

Roasted chicken
- Add colorful vegetables around the chicken

Yule log (bûche de Noël)
- Resembles a cut log
- Add decorations around the base

Christmas decorations

 Candy canes

Stockings

Miniature houses

 Gingerbread men

Santa Claus
- Make a plump belly
- Add a beaming smile for a kindly appearance

105

Infant clothing

Swaddling

Draw the top half of the face.

Make a Y shape to indicate how the fabric is lapped diagonally.

Round off the shape.

Add swaddling behind the head.

Bunting

Draw the head and small hands emerging from sleeves.

Draw a long hem.

Add the snaps.

Onesies

Draw the head with the arms up.

Add diagonal lines for where the legs emerge.

Draw chubby legs in an action pose.

Add the snaps.

[Baby items]

Baby baths
Draw the baby first, and then the bath around it.

Bouncers
Draw a bean shape around the baby, as if loosely wrapping it.

Strollers
Draw it mostly from the side to make it easier.

Mobiles
Draw various decorations dangling from the ends of the rods.

Disposable diapers

Baby bottles
Make sure the nipple is connected to the bottle.

Potty seats

Nursery & elementary schools

Nursery school

School buildings

Make a single-story building with a triangular roof for a realistic look.

Nursery school hats

Turn the brim up.

Small brim
Draw red and white caps for variety.

Nursery school satchels

Start by drawing two overlapping rectangles.

Add a large snap clasp.

Finish by drawing a shoulder strap.

Elementary school

School buildings

Add a clock. Leave the exterior white.

Bucket hats

Brim extends outward all around.

Baseball caps

Backpacks

Start by drawing two curves.

Add the side.

Complete the drawing with shoulder straps.

Graduations

Female graduates

Draw long sleeves.
Show a glimpse
of the fingers.

Mortar boards

Round the top.

Draw a diamond shape.

Finish with color and
a trailing tassel.

Add a ribbon at the
front of the skirt.
Draw a mid-length hem.

Boots complete a
fashionable look.

Male graduates

Draw wide sleeves on the
gown. Add a diamond-
shaped cap.

Diplomas

Long gown
Use the same color for the cap
and the formal graduation gown.

109

Wedding ceremonies

Grooms

Brides

Draw a long
jacket.

Add a large
bouquet.

**Western
style**

Draw hair decorations,
and indicate the
decolletage.

Use triangles to make
the lapels. Indicate a vest
underneath.

Various dress silhouettes

A-line   Mermaid   Princess

Haori and hakama

White kimono

Finish with a trailing hem.

Draw a belt that sits low on the waist.

Draw a folded fan in her hands.

Start by indicating broad shoulders.

Japanese style

Shift the bridal robe off the shoulders.

Show a glimpse of the Japanese hairstyle at the forehead and the sides.

\Congratulations!/

Carp

Gift envelope

Begin with an inverted V inside an incomplete circle.

Symbols

Hospital

Barber shop

Beauty salon

Vaccination

Dentist

Return date

Library

Piano

Hitting the books

Date for collection

Dry cleaning

Soccer

Baseball

Swimming

Karate

English-derived
Japanese words

Watching movies

Study related

Sports related

Watching sports

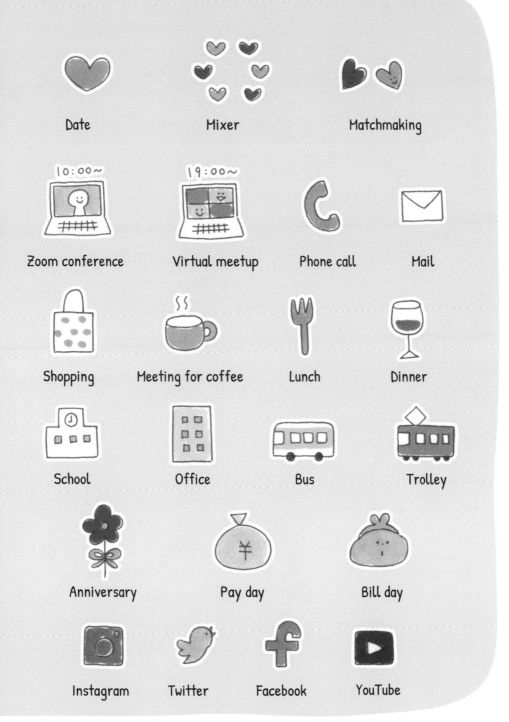

Date

Mixer

Matchmaking

Zoom conference

Virtual meetup

Phone call

Mail

Shopping

Meeting for coffee

Lunch

Dinner

School

Office

Bus

Trolley

Anniversary

Pay day

Bill day

Instagram

Twitter

Facebook

YouTube

Birthdays

Party poppers

Cakes

Party hats

Presents

Message banners

Use these numerals for ages and birthdates!

Fashion

Small fashion items

Shoes

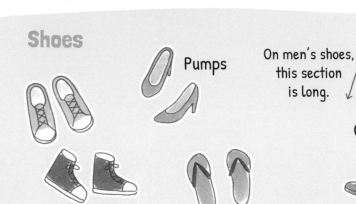

Pumps

On men's shoes, this section is long.

Casual shoes

Sneakers

Flip-flops

Leather shoes

Watches

The watch face is obvious even with no numbers drawn on.

Hats

The key is to draw the shape with eye toward indicating the material.

Different hats

Ski hat with pom poms

Caps

Knitted caps

Hat with a broad brim

Handbags

- There are various types of bags
- Simple ones are the easiest to convey

Eyeglasses

- Change the lenses
- Use a colored pen for the frames if you like

Neckwear

Here are some fashion items for the neck.

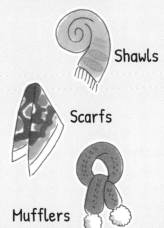

Shawls

Scarfs

Mufflers

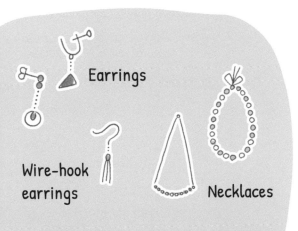

Earrings

Wire-hook earrings

Necklaces

Accessories

It's fun drawing items that are trendy!

117

Festival fashion

Here are some fun fashions that continue traditions.

Jinbei outfits

Lap the front flaps like a kimono in a long Y shape. Keep the sleeves narrow.

Show the tie at the side.

Add knee-length pants.

Hyottoko masks
Pucker the mouth and make the eyes large.

Happi jackets
Make the sleeves short.

Fox masks
Show red markings on a white background. Draw narrow eyes.

Yukata outfits

Start with a short
Y shape at the
neck. The sleeves
are wide.

Position the obi
high on the waist.

Finish the drawing and
add festive colors.

Okame masks

The lower half of the face is plump.

Hannya masks

- Two horns
- Large mouth

Awa Odori festival costumes

- Semi-circular straw hat
- Long sleeves on the kimono

Historical costumes

Here are some fashions that symbolize Japanese culture.

Kofun period

Terracotta funerary figurine

Ancient imperial grave marker

Comma-shaped precious stones

Draw hair in buns next to the ears.

Indicate the wrists and knees bound with cord.

Kofun period
Simple clothing

Nara period
Tang-influenced costumes

Tempyo culture

Drinking vessel

***Biwa* (Japanese lute)**

A person from the Nara period

Draw a bun on the top of the head.

Make wide sleeve openings.

Finish with the long skirt.

Male imperial dress (*sokutai*)

Start with
the lacquered
head piece.

Indicate the
just-visible
kimono collar.

Draw the baton.

Finish with
rounded shoes.

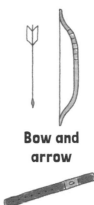

**Bow and
arrow**

Flute

Heian period
Kokufu Bunka dress

Twelve-layered robe (*junihitoe*)

Scroll

Ball

Indicate the
forelocks.

Layer Y
shapes, one
over the other.

Add the fan in
the hand.

Finish with the long-
hemmed skirt, with
the hakama showing
in the center.

121

Historical costumes

Here are fashions for various historical professions.

Warlord

Standard

Spear

Start by drawing the helmet.

Draw armor on the shoulders.

Add the breastplate and sword hilt.

Finish with the legs and add color.

Warring States period

Depending on the family, the horns of the helmet and family crest changed during these turbulent times.

Ninja

Draw a mask that just shows the eyes.

Draw one arm raised.

Indicate the heirloom sword strapped to the back.

Finish by drawing an imposing stance.

Sickle and chain

Throwing stars

Dagger

Samurai

Draw hair on both sides of the head.

Indicate the topknot.

Draw one hand on the sword at the waist, and add a long hakama.

Add the final details and color to finish.

Japanese sword

Oiled-paper umbrella

Edo period
Kimonos are standard.
Use small items to distinguish between individuals.

Courtesan

Start with a Japanese hairstyle.

Add layers.

Show a large obi tied in front.

Finish with a long hem, and add color.

Pipe

Old-fashioned coins

Various ways to hold a pipe

Samurai

Merchant

It can be held like this too

123

Historical costumes

Here are some fashions reflecting events from modern times.

Canteen

Air defense hood

Decorated hats

1940s (wartime)

- Plain clothes for ease of movement

Military uniform

Women's work pants

1950s

- A-line dress with flared skirt
- Distinctive parachute shape

Japanese women's activewear during wartime

Bamboo spear

New look

Flared dress
("parachute dress")

124

Sunglasses and hat that were popular in the 1970s

Shoulder phone

Japan's first cell phone

Pager

Cell phone

1960s
Hippie era

- Expresses a free way of living, embracing love, peace and nature
- Long hair for both men and women

1990s
Bubble era

- Figure is accentuated
- Bold shoulder pads
- Bangs styled like a bird's crest

Psychedelic dress

Go-go boots

Guitar

Form-fitting glamour wear

Feather fan

World costumes

Draw figures in poses that complement outfits symbolizing the culture of various countries and regions.

Northern climes

- Fleecy hat
- Dance with arms crossed

Europe

Depending on the region, draw a skirt with apron, hat, scarf, etc.

Medieval costume

- Princely outfit
- Gentlemanly pose

Middle east

- Turban
- Curved sword held high in the air
- Fierce expression

Africa

- Flamboyant colors
- Various accessories

China
- Cute costume
- Distinctive buttons

Hawaii
- Hula dance
- Gently swaying arms and legs

Draw the distinctive elements for a good result!

South America
- Patterned poncho and hat

South-east Asia
- Baggy pants and flowing scarf
- Bright colors
- Depict with swaying hips and posed hands

Aborigine
- Powerful tribal dance
- Bent knees
- Legs pushed out

Fairytale fashions

Here are some characters that appear in fairy tales.

Angels

- Wings on the back, halo above the head
- Use yellow and gold as key colors

Kings

- Proud stance
- Sumptuously decorated crown and cloak

Princesses

- Small tiara
- Voluminous dress covered in frills

Mounted nobles

- Crown is bigger than a princess's
- Flowing cloak
- A golden flowing tail for the horse increases the air of fantasy

Elves

- Spritely expression
- Slightly pointed ears

Evil spirits

- Pointy wings
- Fangs
- Slightly mischievous expression

Mermaids

- Lower half resembles the tail of a fish
- Long hair
- Don't forget the starfish hair decoration

Pirates

- Peaked hat
- Striped shirt
- Torn pants

Witches

- Triangular hood
- Slightly elongated nose
- Staff is crucial

Cosmetic items

Accouterments that make fashion fun

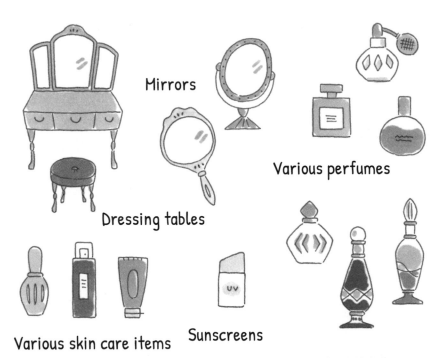

Mirrors

Various perfumes

Dressing tables

Various skin care items

Sunscreens

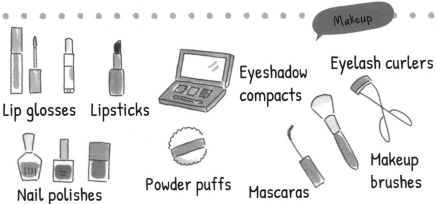

Makeup

Lip glosses

Lipsticks

Eyeshadow compacts

Eyelash curlers

Nail polishes

Powder puffs

Mascaras

Makeup brushes

Houses and Interiors

Things to consider before drawing houses and interiors

 What sort of house are you trying to create?

A modern, streamlined, stylish house?

A cute, fairytale-like house?

A Japanese-style cottage?

 What sort of furniture would you like to put inside?

A stuffed leather sofa?

An antique chair?

A heated table (*kotatsu*)?

 What about other objects?

Visualizing the kind of house you want to portray from the start creates a cohesive interior for a stylish result!

The latest appliances?

Western crockery?

A Showa-era telephone?

External appearance

Outer walls

Windows

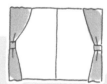

Play with the colors and patterns of the curtains.

Wood lattice

Unique
semi-circle style

Doors

Retro

Apartment type

Mailboxes

Simple type

House-shaped

POST

Toilets

Toilet seats

Draw the back with a straight line.

Draw the front with a rounded line.

Taper the sides downward.

Make the lid large.

Toilet paper

Start with two concentric ovals.

Make the base slightly squared off.

Shade the inside of the roll. Make the torn end of the paper jagged.

Slippers

Curve here.

Toilet brushes

Draw the handle first.

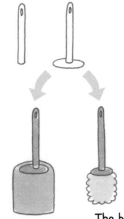

Inside the stand

The brush alone

Bathrooms

Showers

 Draw a wide oval.

 Draw the handle with smooth curves.

Indicate water spray for easy identification.

Shampoo & conditioner bottles

Draw whatever bottle shape you like.　Add the pump component.

Add shampoo and conditioner labels.

Shampoo guards

In use

Basins

Stools

Add a shadows to indicate depth and make the hole more obvious.

First floor living areas

Begin by drawing a large square.

Add the front-loader door and feet.

Draw tumbling clothes and the controls.

Top loader

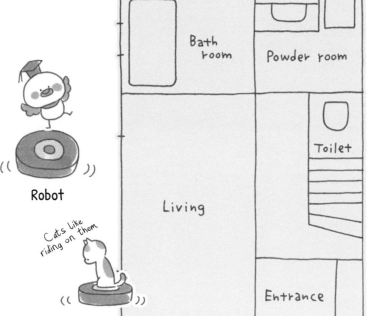

Bath room

Powder room

Toilet

Living

Entrance

Robot

Cats like riding on them

Stick type

Vacuum cleaners

Draw an egg shape with a circle.

Make the wand section straight.

Draw a hose to connect the parts.

Living room furniture

Curtains
Indicate gathers in the fabric.

Sofas
Change the cushions and armrests to create a style you like.

Side tables
Make the closest side longer, and the side farthest away shorter.

Chairs
Create variations by changing the backrest!

Tables
Make the closest legs longer, and the legs farthest away shorter.

Second floor dining rooms and kitchens

Refrigerators

Add a rectangle off to the side and draw in the contents to show an open refrigerator.

Lighting

Change the fixture to suit your taste.

Draw in the floor plan by hand for a cute look.

Kitchen

Dining

Large appliances have similar shapes, so alter how they are drawn to create distinction, such as in the following ways:
- Open a door
- Add small items

Televisions

Remote control

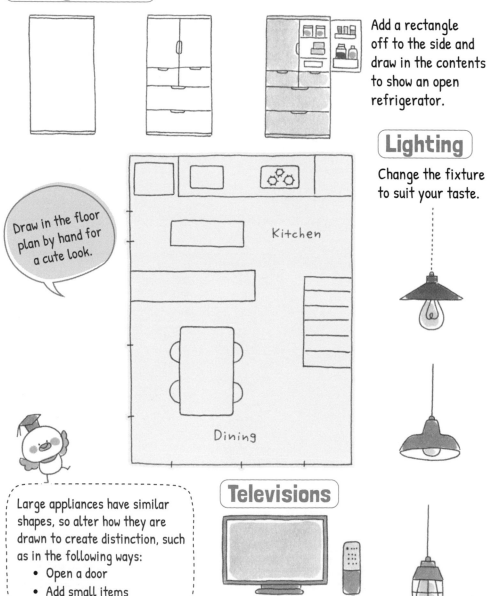

Seasonal appliances

Kerosene heaters

Draw rectangles of different sizes on the top and bottom.

Add vertical lines.

Add the fuel-reservoir base.

Add the control dial and foot.

Place a kettle on it if you like.

You can grill potatoes on it too!

Fans

Draw two concentric circles; make the one in the middle small.

Use just a marker to color in the blades instead of drawing the outline, if you prefer.

Add a long, slender stand.

Draw a sturdy base at the bottom.

It's fine to only color in certain sections.

Kitchen utensils

Rice cookers

Indicate steam if you wish.

Scales

Coffee makers

This is a kitchen with an island.

Kettles

Gas ranges

Cutting boards and knives

Crockery · Create your own designs

Plates

Draw ones you'd like to have for yourself!

Small bowls

Coffee cups

Depending on the colors, they can look modern or refined.

Cutlery

Storage containers

Enameled vessels

Butter dishes

Teapots

Pots

Pot shapes vary depending on their purpose. Draw ones that suit what you like to cook.

Frying pans

Third floor bedrooms and personal spaces

Chairs

Draw the frame, curtains and bed, in that order.

Four-poster beds

Bunk beds

Single beds

Kidsroom

Study

Bed room

Visualize a 3D rectangle.　　Flesh in the mattress.　　Draw the headboard.

Home office-related items

Notebook computers

There's no need to draw individual keys in detail.

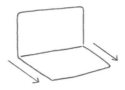

| Make the screen rather wide. | Make the sides of the base diagonal. | Draw the display and the keyboard. |

All-in-one printers

| Start by drawing a trapezoid. | Add a substantial rectangular face. | Accessorize with buttons, display, etc. |

How about these?

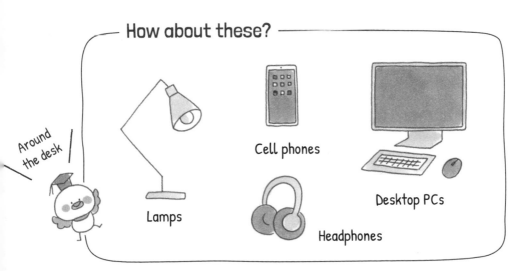

Around the desk

Lamps

Cell phones

Headphones

Desktop PCs

On the desk

Benitengu

Sakuratake

Favorite photos

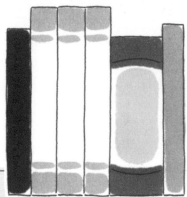

Books

Pencil cases

Tape rolls

Stamps

Protractors

Rulers

Set squares

Tape measures

Binder clips

Inks

Fountain pens

Paper clips

Glue products

Bulldog clips

Various pens

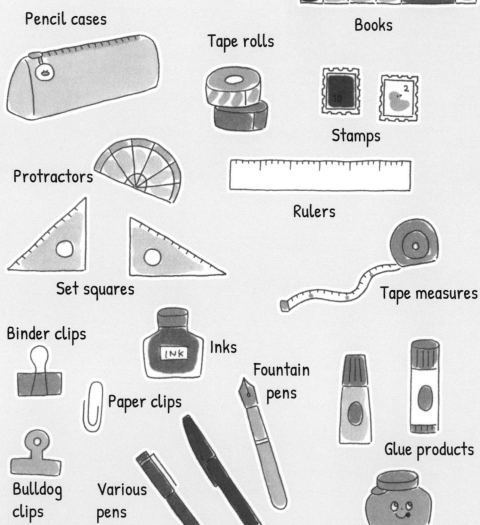

Cutting/Gluing

Scissors

Draw a "b" on an angle.

Add a long blade.

Add another "b."

Open scissors

When you want to draw a simple scissors motif such as for indicating a cutting line, just draw two circles and lines!

Closed scissors

Box cutters

Start with two long, thin rectangles.

Add lines.

Indicate a button for moving the blade.

Draw a diagonal blade and add color.

Scotch tape dispensers

Draw a small valley and large mountain.

Square it off.

Draw the visible part of the roll.

Add the spindle and tape extending to the blade.

Writing utensils

For pens and pencils, create variations on long, thin rectangles.

Pencils

Mechanical pencils

Ballpoint pens

Markers

The tips differentiate each type

Thin line

Triangular

Rounded

Make the edge of the painted barrel jagged for a sharpened pencil.

Eraser tip

Retractable pens with various colors

Make the nib trapezoidal for highlighters and the like.

Colored pencils

146

Paper items

 For paper items, create variations on rectangles.

Clear folders

Notebooks

Spiral-bound notebooks

Paper with the corner turned up

Join two pieces to make an opened notebook. Round the tops to create a supple look.

Round the corners. Add rings at the top for a memo pad.

Various thicknesses

Differentiate between book types by thickness.

Draw a little of the page edges to make 3D.

Add a little more thickness for a book.

Make a dictionary even thicker.

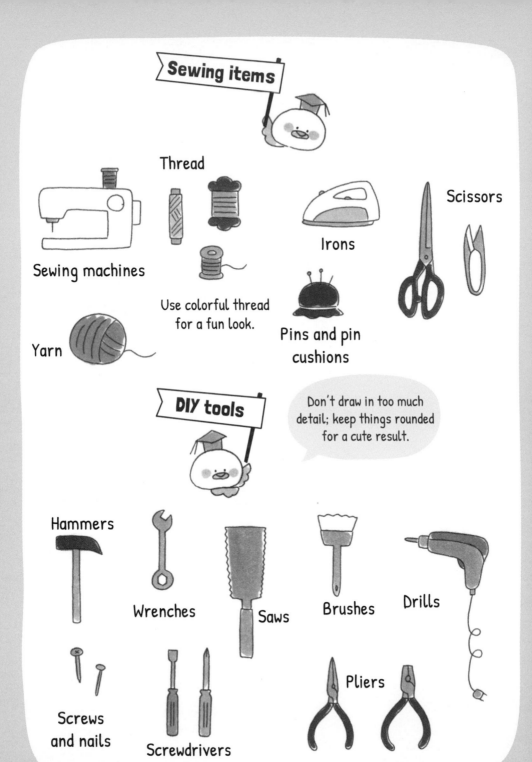

Sewing items

Thread

Sewing machines

Use colorful thread for a fun look.

Irons

Pins and pin cushions

Scissors

Yarn

DIY tools

Don't draw in too much detail; keep things rounded for a cute result.

Hammers

Wrenches

Saws

Brushes

Drills

Screws and nails

Screwdrivers

Pliers

Vehicles

Trains

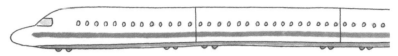

Bullet trains

- Slender front section
- Small windows and wheels
- It's easiest to draw a side view

Trains

- Combine rectan-gles and circles
- Change the colors to depict different routes

Steam locomotives

- The circle at the front and the smokestack are important details
- Colors such as gray and burgundy work nicely

Street cars

- Similar to a train but shorter
- Make it rounded for a retro look

Familiar city vehicles

Firetrucks

The cab is essentially a square; make the front window diagonal.

Draw a rectangle for the back.

Add windows and a light. Add a spiral for the hose.

Add a ladder on top, and color the truck red.

Ambulances

Essentially rectangular; make the front window diagonal.

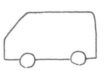

Add tires.

Add lights at the front and back.

Add a red stripe.

Police cars

Extend the sides of a trapezoid.

Connect at the base and add tires and windows.

Add the light on top.

Color the lower half gray.

Vehicles used on construction sites

Cranes

Add a rectangle and four circles off to the side.

Begin with a modified rectangular shape; make the front window diagonal.

Add the platform at the back.

Extend the arm and add a hook.

Keep the distinctive features simple!

Here, the dump truck is shown offloading its burden.

Add sand or some other load.

Add an L-shaped truck bed.

Start with a truck similar to the crane, above.

Dump trucks

Begin by drawing a long oval with two circles inside. Place a rectangular platform on top.

Add another platform on top.

Draw a forward-facing curved section, and then diagonal lines that slope downward.

Finish by drawing a large semicircular shovel.

Finish with a small exhaust pipe. Add lights and other details.

Draw the cabin on top.

Begin by drawing two straight lines, top and bottom, joined by curves on the sides.

Add the caterpillar belt at the side using an oval with two circles inside.

Bulldozers

153

Carnival rides

Merry-go-rounds

Begin by drawing a triangular roof and add a decorative frill.

Add two vertical lines underneath to form a thick central column.

Draw a long rectangular platform for the base.

Add horses.

Add poles and color.

Ferris wheels

Roller coaster
Exaggeratedly steep tracks create just the right look.

Draw large, medium and small concentric circles.

Create a triangle for the base.

Divide the wheel into about eight equal parts.

Add small circles at the ends for the gondolas. Use festive colors for a lively effect.

Fantasy

Don't get bogged down by details, just make sure distinctive features are clear.

Pirate ships

Make the prow long.
Add ocean waves.

Add a mast with a sail
and banner at the front.

Draw a large mast and
sail in the middle.

Add a sail at the back
about the same size
as the one in front.

Add a skull motif to
the large sail.

Pumpkin carriages

Start by making an oval in the center
and add lobes that swell out at the sides.

Add the stem to
complete a pumpkin.

Draw the window and vine
Add a slight bump at
the bottom.

Add wheels at the
front and back.

Add details and
color to finish.

Familiar modes of transportation

Bicycles

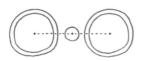

Draw two large sets of concentric circles, with one small circle in between.

Join the circles with lines.

Add a line for the handlebars.

Add the saddle, pedals and hand grips.

Add a basket and color to finish.

Buses

Draw a rectangular body with a rectangular door.

Draw lots of windows.

Add a bus stop marker for a realistic look.

Frequently seen vehicles

Taxi

Post office van

Courier van

Draw lines and rectangles for the handlebars.

Draw a large tire in front.

Join the parts.

Add a saddle.

Draw the small tire at the back.

Add in the tire that's farthest away.

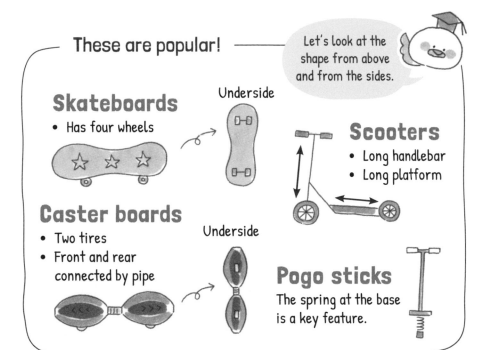

These are popular!

Let's look at the shape from above and from the sides.

Skateboards

Underside

- Has four wheels

Scooters

- Long handlebar
- Long platform

Caster boards

Underside

- Two tires
- Front and rear connected by pipe

Pogo sticks

The spring at the base is a key feature.

Transportation from olden times

This is how it was carried.

Palanquins

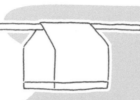

Draw a pole passing through a steepled shape.

Complete the house-like shape.

Add windows and other decorations.

Rickshaws

Draw a big wheel and the roof.

Add the seat and draw in the footrest.

It was pulled like this.

Add lines to indicate three-dimensionality.

Add decorations and the long poles.

Architecture

Houses of the world

[Sweden]
Red house

Summer version

Winter version

[Norway]
Grass roof

[Mongolia]
Yurt

[Greece]
**Made from
mortar and stone**

[Turkey]
Cave dwelling

[Iran]
Windcatcher

[Canada]
Brightly painted
wooden structures

[Japan]
Traditional
thatched
house

[Japan]
Traditional
house

[Hawaii]
Ancient
grass house

[Thailand]
Stilted structures
on the river

[Philippines]
Stilted houses
on the beach

Houses of the world
vary in functionality
and design.

Buildings in Tokyo

Shrines

Start with the peak
of the roof that
turns up at the ends.

Draw a
broad roof.

Add columns.

Add in horizontal beams.

Finish by adding a
large red lantern.

Tokyo Dome

Begin by drawing
the roof as a long
leaf shape.

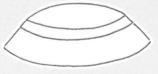

Broaden the roof at
the base.

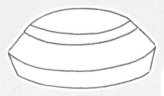

Taper the walls.

Indicate columns.

Add areas of color.

Tokyo Station

Round out the entryway at the center.

Draw a trapezoidal roof.

Add pillars to the sides.

Extend structures out to the sides.

Add lots of windows.

Various towers

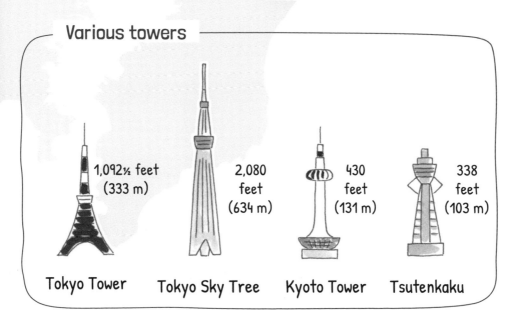

Tokyo Tower — 1,092½ feet (333 m)

Tokyo Sky Tree — 2,080 feet (634 m)

Kyoto Tower — 430 feet (131 m)

Tsutenkaku — 338 feet (103 m)

Buildings in the Kansai/ Chugoku region

Kinkakuji (Golden Pavilion)

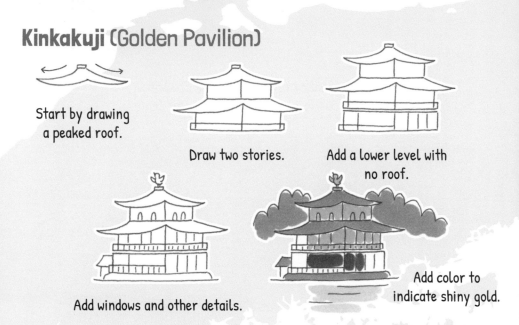

Start by drawing a peaked roof.

Draw two stories.

Add a lower level with no roof.

Add windows and other details.

Add color to indicate shiny gold.

Itsukushima Shrine Torii

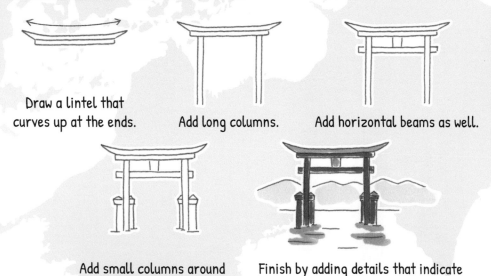

Draw a lintel that curves up at the ends.

Add long columns.

Add horizontal beams as well.

Add small columns around the structure.

Finish by adding details that indicate the shrine's position in the sea.

Himeji Castle (Also known as White Heron Castle)

Start by drawing a rounded arch in the middle of the top story.

Add a story beneath with a triangular roof feature.

Add a story beneath with a two triangular roof features.

Add two trapezoids around the base.

The walls of the castle are white.

Horyuji Five-storied Pagoda

Begin at the top with a triangle and a rectangle.

Make four levels.

Make a large rectangular area underneath the fifth layer from the top.

Draw the base.

Add color and the decorative feature on the top.

Buildings in the Kyushu/ Okinawa region

Mojiko Station

- Neo-Renaissance-style Western building made from wood.

Black outer walls

[Kumamoto prefecture]
Kumamoto Castle
(also known as Ginkgo Castle)

- One of the three great castles in Japan
- It gets its alternate name from the large ginkgo tree in the main courtyard

Long narrow rocket

[Kagoshima prefecture]
Tanegashima Space Center

- Large rocket launch site

[Okinawa prefecture]
Shuri Castle

- A fusion of Japanese and Chinese architectural styles
- Distinctive use of color

Buildings in the Hokkaido/Tohoku region

[Hokkaido]
Sapporo Clock Tower

- Built as the Sapporo Agricultural College performance hall
- The triangular roofs in the center are key

Simplified to a three-arch span in the illustration

[Iwate prefecture]
Chūson-ji Temple

- A Buddhist temple from the Heian period, completely gold in color

[Iwate prefecture]
Megane Bridge

- Bridge said to be the motif of Kenji Miyazawa's *Night on the Galactic Railroad*

The red hall is the oldest structure on the mountain

[Yamagata prefecture]
Risshakuji Temple

- Famous for Matsuo Basho's haiku:
  ah, the silence
  sinking into the rocks
  the voice of the cicada

Structures that symbolize various countries

Statue of Liberty

Draw a torch held in the right hand with the right arm raised beside the head.

Add the long robe.

Show the tablet in the left hand.

Add the pedestal beneath the feet.

Finish with the spikes protruding from the crown.

Great Wall of China

Begin by drawing the face of the meandering wall.

Add a watchtower entrance.

Fill in the rest of the watchtower.

Extend the road atop the wall into the distance.

Use a cloud to conceal the receding wall in the background.

The Great Sphinx and pyramids at Giza

It's fine to use lines for the nose and mouth.

The squarish brow defines the face.

Draw the human upper body and the feet of a lion.

Add angular shapes to either side of the face.

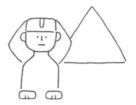

Place a triangular pyramid in the background.

Use lines and dots to indicate architecture built from sandstone blocks.

Chichen Itza

Begin at the top with a squarish entrance.

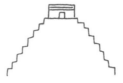

Add jagged steps on both sides.

Make the overall shape triangular.

Add stairs running up the center.

Add color appropriate for stone ruins.

Taj Mahal

Begin by drawing the onion-shaped dome above an open rectangle.

Add small onion-shaped domes on either side.

Add open trapezoids to the sides to create a sense of depth.

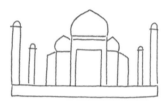 

Draw four minarets. Make the two that are farthest away smaller.

Indicate the platforms and other details.

St. Basil's Cathedral

Draw an onion-domed tower.

Add 2 smaller towers.

Add 2 more large towers.

Draw a large cone at the back, and small triangles to one side and in front.

A platform for the base creates a cohesive look.

Add color and decorative details to finish.

Sagrada Familia

Start by drawing
rounded triangles.

Add four longer
triangles at the back.

Decorate the tops.

Add jagged-roofed
buildings at the sides.

Color the whole
structure light brown.

Mont-Saint-Michel

Begin by drawing
the tallest tower
in the middle.

Extend the structure
out to the sides.

Extend the
structure below.

Make puffy shapes for
the trees.

Draw the island
with buildings
here and there.

Leaning Tower of Pisa

Draw an open
rectangle on an angle.

Adding the horizon line
makes things clearer.

Use lines to
define the levels.

Make a decorative arched
entrance on the bottom floor.

Draw a fluttering
flag on top.

St. Paul's Cathedral

Begin by drawing what
looks like a house with
a triangular roof.

Add rectangular
structures at the sides.

Draw a large rectangular
structure in the back.

Add a dome and lighthouse-
like structure on top.

Extend structures far out to the
sides and add touches of color.

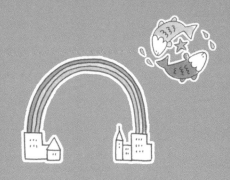

Weather, Seasons and Planets

Weather

Fair

Blazing heat

Gentle sunshine

Cloudy

Occasional sun

Light showers

Rain

Heavy rain

Tropical storm

Snow

Blizzard

Heavy snowfall

174

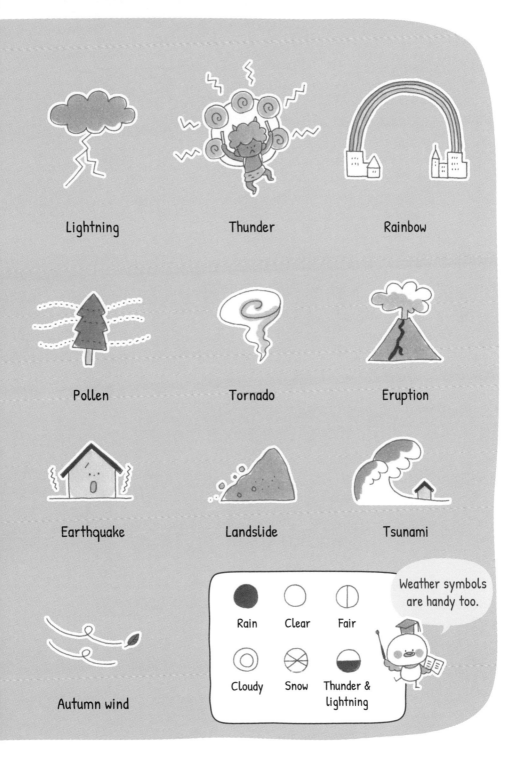

Lightning

Thunder

Rainbow

Pollen

Tornado

Eruption

Earthquake

Landslide

Tsunami

Autumn wind

Rain   Clear   Fair

Cloudy   Snow   Thunder & lightning

Weather symbols are handy too.

Scorpio

Libra

Virgo

Leo

Sagittarius

Cancer

Twelve zodiac signs

Capricorn

Gemini

Taurus

Pisces

Aquarius

Aries

Seasons in the mountains (Spring)

- Vibrant yellows and pinks
- Green color for bright new sprouts

Mountain vegetables

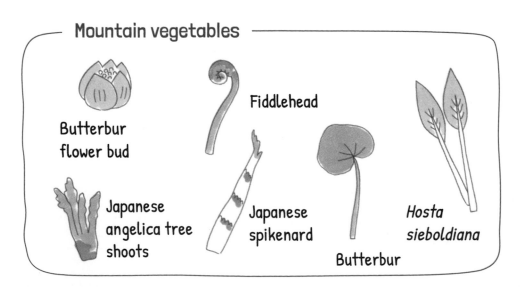

Butterbur
flower bud

Fiddlehead

Japanese
angelica tree
shoots

Japanese
spikenard

Butterbur

*Hosta
sieboldiana*

Seasons in the mountains (Summer)

- Plenty of greenery and fresh color
- Cumulonimbus clouds evoke summer, so it's good to show them

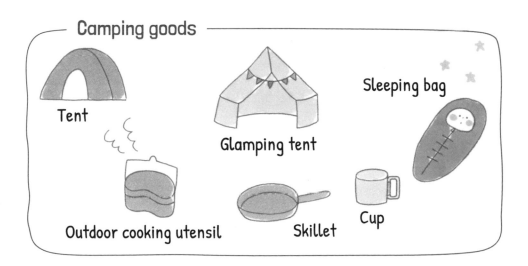

Camping goods

Tent

Glamping tent

Sleeping bag

Outdoor cooking utensil

Skillet

Cup

Seasons in the mountains (Fall)

- Leaves turn colors such as red and yellow
- Fall colors throughout

Fallen leaves, etc.

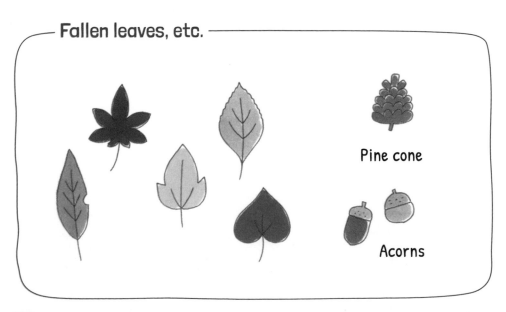

Pine cone

Acorns

Seasons in the mountains (Winter)

- Snowy landscape
- Draw in occasional tree trunks and branches

Winter sports

Igloo

Hare with
winter coat

Snowboarder

Skis

Skates

Seasons at the seaside (Summer)

- Create contrast for a cheerful atmosphere
- Use vivid color for beach items to create a summery feel

Traditional beach items for summer

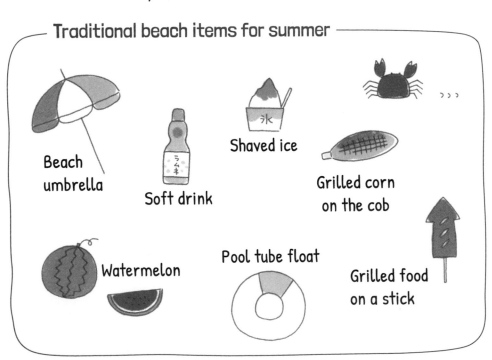

Beach umbrella

Soft drink

Shaved ice

Grilled corn on the cob

Watermelon

Pool tube float

Grilled food on a stick

Seasons at the seaside (Winter)

- Monochromatic color scheme throughout
- Long horizontal clouds create the look of a windswept sky

Traditional beach items for winter

Collect and observe the flotsam and jetsam that washes up on the beach.

Beachcombing

Message in a bottle

Lighthouse

Surfer

Seagull

Clouds and shadows

Use Copic markers for a soft-edged look.

Create the look of a heap of clouds
Cumulonimbus clouds

Make long white lines
Contrails

Lots of small clouds
Altocumulus clouds

Use different tones of the same color
Rain clouds

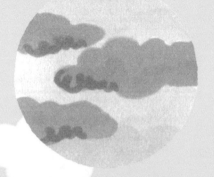

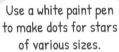

Use a white paint pen to make dots for stars of various sizes.

Use orange and yellow to make shadows
Evening clouds

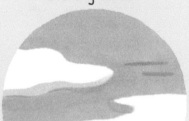

Layered, blended color
Milky Way

Sun and shadow

Adding shadow gives the impression of strong or harsh sunlight. Use it to create contrast, such as for midsummer scenes.

Add a shadow to create a backlit effect.

Moon and planets

Ruled Lines, Letters and Borders

Master the basics (Ways to decorate lines)

Repeat the same illustration in a pattern.

Ways to thicken letters

Basically thicken vertical strokes, but for hiragana and kanji, prioritize balance over rules!

English letters

Make either vertical stroke thick For a single word.

AGAIN

Be consistent with repeated letters.

N H M

For straight letters, thickening both sides creates balance.

Slight protrusions look stylish!

A B F

Hiragana

First, thicken the obvious vertical stroke.

Thicken any areas that seem too thin.

Adjust to achieve balance.

Kanji

Thicken the key stroke.

Emphasize the line and dot.

Keeping the overall balance in mind, thicken the rest of the character.

189

All-rounders: characters with thick vertical lines

A B C D E F G H I
J K L M N O P Q R
S T U V W X Y Z ?

a b c d e f g h i
j k l m n o p q r
s t u v w x y z !

1 2 3 4 5 6 7 8 9 0 ;

Variations

GOOD thank you!

あいうえお　かきくけこ
さしすせそ　たちつてと
なにぬねの　はひふへほ
まみむめも　や　ゆ　よ
らりるれろ　わ　を　ん

アイウエオ　カキクケコ
サシスセソ　タチツテト
ナニヌネノ　ハヒフヘホ
マミムメモ　ヤ　ユ　ヨ
ラリルレロ　ワ。ヲヮン

Double lines and gaps are key

Double line characters

A B C D E F G H I

J K L M N O P Q R

S T U V W X Y Z ?

a b c d e f g h i

j k l m n o p q r

s t u v w x y z !

1 2 3 4 5 6 7 8 9 0 ;

Variations

HELLO Thank you

あいうえお　かきくけこ
さしすせそ　たちつてと
なにぬねの　はひふへほ
まみむめも　や　ゆ　よ
らりるれろ　わ　を　ん

アイウエオ　カキクケコ
サシスセソ　タチツテト
ナニヌネノ　ハヒフヘホ
マミムメモ　ヤ　ユ　ヨ
ラリルレロ　ワ ヮ ヲ。ン

Curly characters

A B C D E F G H I
J K L M N O P Q R
S T U Y W X Y Z ?

a b c d e f g h i
j k l m n o p q r
s t u v w x y z !

1 2 3 4 5 6 7 8 9 0 ;

Variations

Happy Birthday!   Thank you!

Japanese and retro-style Japanese characters

あ い う え お　か き く け こ
さ し す せ そ　た ち つ て と
な に ぬ ね の　は ひ ふ へ ほ
ま み む め も　や　ゆ　よ
ら り る れ ろ　わ　を　ん

ア イ ウ エ オ　カ キ ク ケ コ
サ シ ス セ ソ　タ チ ッ テ ト
ナ 二 ヌ ネ ノ　ハ ヒ フ ヘ ホ
マ ミ ム メ モ　ヤ　エ　ヨ
テ リ ル レ ロ　ヴ 。 ヲ ゛ ン

Frequently used English phrases

Add letters and words to illustrations, make combinations, and so on.

Speech bubbles
Creating depth makes for a pop-art look.

Birthdays
Write a birthday message inside a decorated cake.

Greetings
Use auspicious colors and items.

Thanks
Write your sentiments on a banner.

Reverse type
Outline the letters first, and then color the background.

Add line and color in various places on the letters.

Characters that match illustrations
Give the drawings and letters a sense of thematic unity.

Use illustration for part of the phrase
One letter in "home" is an illustration.

Turn the phrase into a design
Use the color and shape to spark ideas.

Combine different designs and typefaces
Using different designs for each word creates emphasis when you really want to get something across.

Frequently used Japanese phrases

あけまして
おめでとう
ございます

Keep the number of characters consistent

If using hiragana, sometimes the number of characters conveniently lines up. Try making use of this in the design.

新 謹
年 賀

Arrange in a square

Put one character into each quadrant of a square design.

賀
正

Add text inside the illustration

Place a phrase inside a suitable illustration.

Change the illustration according to the Chinese zodiac year.

One character in each section

Add one character to each part of the illustration.

メ
リ ー ク リ ス マ ス

Add a floral illustration around the phrase

Arranging seasonal flowers around the outside demonstrates your sense of style.

Turn the border into an illustration

A version where the phrase is inside a border-turned-illustration.

Characters' speech bubbles

Creating the look of characters' speech makes for an adorable effect.

Doodles that are the message

Incorporate the phrase itself into the illustration for a cute look.

Borders

Tone down the use of color to make the letters stand out.

- Add key words or phrases
- Use handwriting to create a sense of warmth

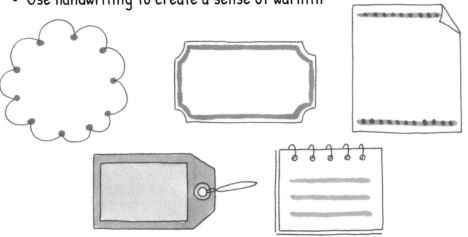

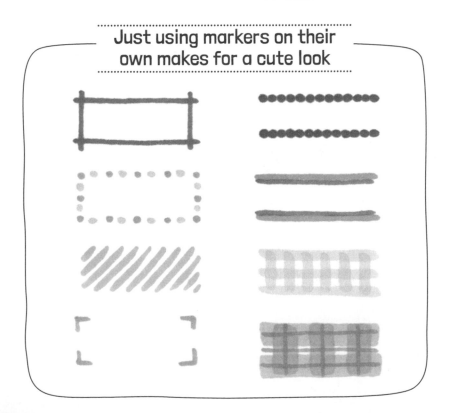

Just using markers on their own makes for a cute look

Creating Characters

What sort of character will you make?
Visualize it as you sketch!

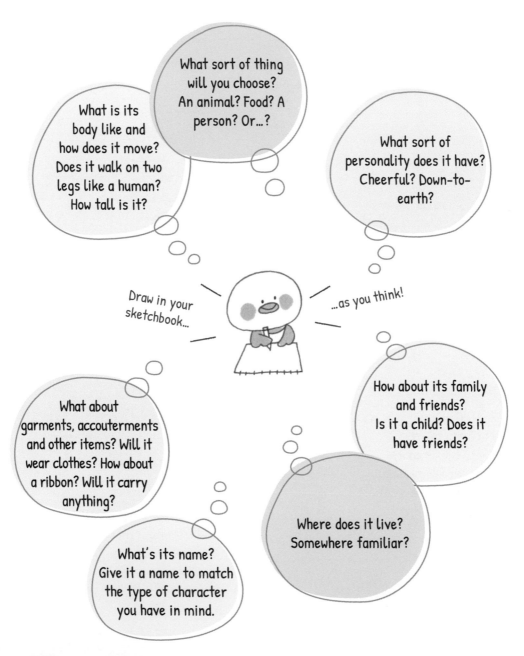

What sort of thing will you choose? An animal? Food? A person? Or...?

What is its body like and how does it move? Does it walk on two legs like a human? How tall is it?

What sort of personality does it have? Cheerful? Down-to-earth?

Draw in your sketchbook...

...as you think!

What about garments, accouterments and other items? Will it wear clothes? How about a ribbon? Will it carry anything?

How about its family and friends? Is it a child? Does it have friends?

Where does it live? Somewhere familiar?

What's its name? Give it a name to match the type of character you have in mind.

Sketch in the distinctive features

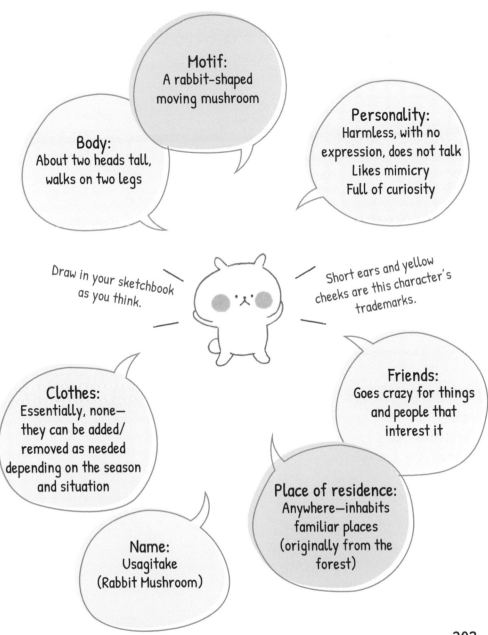

Motif:
A rabbit-shaped
moving mushroom

Body:
About two heads tall,
walks on two legs

Personality:
Harmless, with no
expression, does not talk
Likes mimicry
Full of curiosity

Draw in your sketchbook
as you think.

Short ears and yellow
cheeks are this character's
trademarks.

Clothes:
Essentially, none—
they can be added/
removed as needed
depending on the season
and situation

Friends:
Goes crazy for things
and people that
interest it

Place of residence:
Anywhere—inhabits
familiar places
(originally from the
forest)

Name:
Usagitake
(Rabbit Mushroom)

Try drawing various expressions and poses for the character you've created!

Once the character's personality is decided, its expressions and movements become clear, so put yourself in the character's shoes and think how you would act in certain situations in order to pose it.

Basic posture
A well-mannered character

Rear view
Largeish tail

Jumping
This character's coordination is also good

Side profile
Tummy sticks out

Sleeping
Closes eyes when sleeping

Downcast
Ears droop when feeling down

Usagitake's expressions are limitless!

Raincoat

Umbrella

Futon

Usagitake covets other people's things, so it just makes those things its own!

Mask

Stuck on with tape

Usagitake's own face is the motif on the mask!

Happy

Eyes sparkle when happy

Eating

Mouth only opens when eating

[Main colors]

On the next pages I'll show you a bit of the background to Usagitake's creation.

I actually came up with the prototype for Usagitake when I was in high school. Since then, I've made various changes to get it to its current form. Of course, it's fine to create a character that's perfectly formed from the start! However, it's also possible to take time and develop it gradually, and I think it's meaningful to enjoy its creation in this manner.

The creation of Usagitake

Usagitake: first generation

When I was in high school, I was in the art club.

Mochi that we grilled on the heater in the club's room ↓

I started sketching the first generation of Usagitake.

The manga I liked at the time →

The supervising teacher liked mushrooms, so...

Really?

Can you eat this?

This is fine.

What is this?

...mushrooms became familiar to us.

On a club trip we ate a stew of mystery mushrooms

I really didn't get oil painting, sculpture and so on.

Terrible work

This is how you do it!

Look, you have a try.

Oh, right.

If I could do it, then I would.

I could draw Usagitake.

Wow, so you can draw things like that!

Um... I can draw these...

Then, life got busy and I put Usagitake on hold for a while.

One day it was decided that I'd appear on kids' TV.

Why don't you upload one illustration per day?

← Co-performer

Yes! I'll do that!

Submissive when capable of the task

Nervous

All you have to do for Instagram is take a photo, so it's easy, don't you think?

Yes, yes!

↖ That's simple!

So with that in mind...

I started posting illustrations to Instagram

For a while, I was uploading illustrations other than Usagitake.

Snap!

One day...

Hey...something looks different.

Oh!

Enter Usagitake!

At the time, Instagram only allowed one picture per post, so I decided to draw a crowd of Usagitake to really make an impact!

©kamo.

They just kept increasing, and now here I am today.

Now the face is basically a circle.

The more I drew, the fatter Usagitake became, and the shorter the ears got.

kamo.

This is Kamo's method!

\ Hand-drawn version /

Upload to Instagram for lots of views

1 Once you've drawn the picture...

2 ...Take it near a window and take a photo.

It's bright here

Snap!

3 Log into Instagram.

4 [+] Select the photo (illustration) and edit.

▶ To upload multiple pictures in the one post, select this icon: ▢

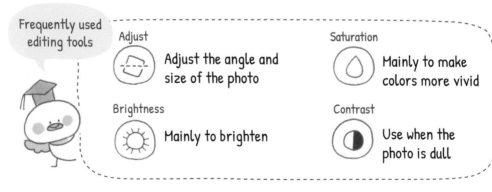

Frequently used editing tools

Adjust
Adjust the angle and size of the photo

Saturation
Mainly to make colors more vivid

Brightness
Mainly to brighten

Contrast
Use when the photo is dull

5 Add a caption and hashtags and post

Adding a # allows you to search for posts with the same hashtag, so it's convenient. Don't forget your character's name!

For example: #usagitake

Create character merchandise!

There are various items that you can create, even as an individual. A lot of them require transferring data, but it's great to see your character come to life. It's definitely worth giving it a try!

Stickers

A sticker sold on my LINE online store page. Individuals can produce and sell their own items if they go through the process of production, application and screening.
https://store.line.me/stickershop/product/1649455/ja

Standing to attention

Looking up

Washi tape

There was a call for masking tape production (not to sell) and I applied. Many people said they wanted it. We received a lot of requests!

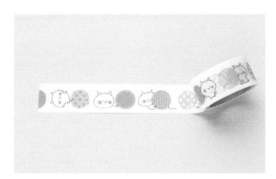

Buttons

I created these as special prizes in the "Usagitake challenge" (not for sale). It was fun working with the circular design.

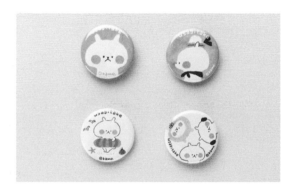

Try making a picture book! Start by making mini sketches

Back cover (page 12)

Front cover (page 1)

Page 2

Page 3

Page 4

Page 5

First, look in a book shop or library to find the style of book you want to emulate. Start by making note of the size of the book, size of the pictures, amount of text, number of colors and so on.

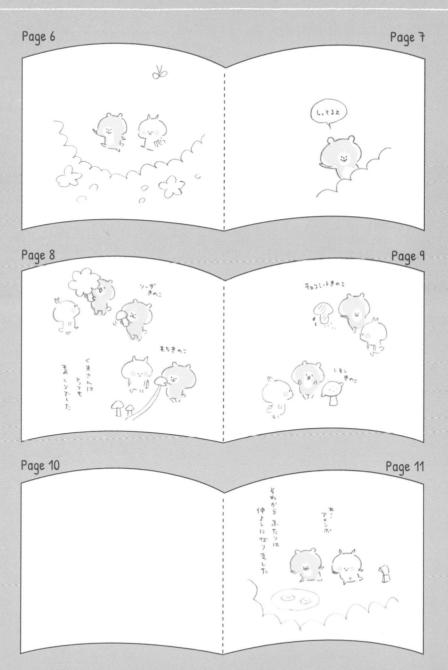

Think about the cover of the picture book! First, decide what to draw

The cover can be considered to be the "face" of the book. It's fine to use illustrations from inside the book or other options. One thing I can say is that the cover illustration needs to be something that will generate interest and make the viewer want to open the book.

I colored motifs from the forest where Usagitake and the bear met and used them to create a border. ♡

T

"Books to Span the East and West"

Tuttle Publishing was founded in 1832 in the small New England town of Rutland, Vermont [USA]. Our core values remain as strong today as they were then—to publish best-in-class books which bring people together one page at a time. In 1948, we established a publishing office in Japan—and Tuttle is now a leader in publishing English-language books about the arts, languages and cultures of Asia. The world has become a much smaller place today and Asia's economic and cultural influence has grown. Yet the need for meaningful dialogue and information about this diverse region has never been greater. Over the past seven decades, Tuttle has published thousands of books on subjects ranging from martial arts and paper crafts to language learning and literature—and our talented authors, illustrators, designers and photographers have won many prestigious awards. We welcome you to explore the wealth of information available on Asia at www.tuttlepublishing.com.

Published by Tuttle Publishing, an imprint of Periplus Editions (HK) Ltd.

www.tuttlepublishing.com

ISBN 978-4-8053-1701-3

Kamo San No Illust Daihyakka
Copyright © 2021 KAMO
Copyright © 2021 GENKOSHA CO., Ltd.
All rights reserved.
English translation rights arranged with
GENKOSHA CO., Ltd. through
Japan UNI Agency, Inc., Tokyo

English translation © 2023 Periplus Editions (HK) Ltd
Translated from Japanese by Leeyong Soo

Printed in Singapore   2210TP
27 26 25 24 23   10 9 8 7 6 5 4 3 2 1

Distributed by:

North America, Latin America & Europe
Tuttle Publishing
364 Innovation Drive
North Clarendon
VT 05759-9436 U.S.A.
Tel: (802) 773-8930; Fax: (802) 773-6993
info@tuttlepublishing.com
www.tuttlepublishing.com

Japan
Tuttle Publishing
Yaekari Building 3rd Floor
5-4-12 Osaki Shinagawa-ku
Tokyo 141 0032
Tel: (81) 3 5437-0171; Fax: (81) 3 5437-0755
sales@tuttle.co.jp
www.tuttle.co.jp

Asia Pacific
Berkeley Books Pte. Ltd.
3 Kallang Sector, #04-01
Singapore 349278
Tel: (65) 6741-2178; Fax: (65) 6741-2179
inquiries@periplus.com.sg
www.tuttlepublishing.com